A SUMMER STORM AT ORGAN PIPE CACTUS NATIONAL MONUMENT

SAGUAROS AND CHOLLAS AT SUNSET IN THE SANTA CATALINAS

BRITTLEBUSH AND BARREL CACTI IN THE PINACATE REGION

LUPINE EDGED BY BRITTLEBUSH IN THE MAZATZAL MOUNTAINS

SAGUARO NATIONAL MONUMENT UNDER A RARE SNOW BLANKET

THE PALOVERDE, ARIZONA'S STATE TREE

EL GRAN DESIERTO OF MEXICO UNDER A LOWERING SKY

Other Publications:

LIBRARY OF HEALTH
CLASSICS OF THE OLD WEST
THE EPIC OF FLIGHT
THE GOOD COOK
THE SEAFARERS
THE ENCYCLOPEDIA OF COLLECTIBLES
THE GREAT CITIES
WORLD WAR II
HOME REPAIR AND IMPROVEMENT
THE WORLD'S WILD PLACES
THE TIME-LIFE LIBRARY OF BOATING
HUMAN BEHAVIOR
THE ART OF SEWING
THE OLD WEST
THE EMERGENCE OF MAN
THE TIME-LIFE ENCYCLOPEDIA OF GARDENING
LIFE LIBRARY OF PHOTOGRAPHY
THIS FABULOUS CENTURY
FOODS OF THE WORLD
TIME-LIFE LIBRARY OF AMERICA
TIME-LIFE LIBRARY OF ART
GREAT AGES OF MAN
LIFE SCIENCE LIBRARY
THE LIFE HISTORY OF THE UNITED STATES
TIME READING PROGRAM
LIFE NATURE LIBRARY
LIFE WORLD LIBRARY
FAMILY LIBRARY:
    HOW THINGS WORK IN YOUR HOME
    THE TIME-LIFE BOOK OF THE FAMILY CAR
    THE TIME-LIFE FAMILY LEGAL GUIDE
    THE TIME-LIFE BOOK OF FAMILY FINANCE

This volume is one of a series that explores the wild regions of the United States, the Caribbean, Mexico and Central America.

CACTUS COUNTRY

THE AMERICAN WILDERNESS/TIME-LIFE BOOKS/ALEXANDRIA, VIRGINIA

BY EDWARD ABBEY
AND THE EDITORS OF TIME-LIFE BOOKS

THE AMERICAN WILDERNESS
Editorial Staff for *Cactus Country*
EDITOR: Charles Osborne
Text Editor: Harvey B. Loomis
Picture Editor: Mary Y. Steinbauer
Designer: Charles Mikolaycak
Staff Writer: Gerald Simons
Chief Researcher: Martha T. Goolrick
Researchers: Joan Chambers, Angela Dews,
Barbara Ensrud, Rhea Finkelstein, Helen M. Hinkle,
Beatrice Hsia, Gillian McManus
Design Assistant: Mervyn Clay

Revisions Staff
SENIOR EDITOR: Rosalind Stubenberg
Text Editor: Lee Greene
Researcher: Ellen Keir
Copy Coordinator: Cynthia Kleinfeld
Picture Coordinator: Jane A. Martin
Editorial Assistants: Mary Kosak, Linda Yates
Art Assistant: Jeanne Potter

EDITORIAL OPERATIONS
Production Director: Feliciano Madrid
   Assistants: Peter A. Inchauteguiz, Karen A. Meyerson
Copy Processing: Gordon E. Buck
Quality Control Director: Robert L. Young
   Assistant: James J. Cox
   Associates: Daniel J. McSweeney, Michael G. Wight
Art Coordinator: Anne B. Landry
Copy Room Director: Susan B. Galloway
   Assistants: Celia Beattie, Ricki Tarlow

The Author: Edward Abbey has lived in the American
Southwest since 1947. He has written several books on
the region, including *Desert Solitaire, The Journey Home*
and *Abbey's Road.*

The Consultant: Mervin W. Larson, formerly Director of the
Arizona-Sonora Desert Museum near Tucson, has collabo-
rated with his wife, Peggy, on four books dealing with deserts and the behavior of social insects.

The Cover: Giant saguaros, the largest species of cactus in
Arizona, stand in silhouette against a desert sunset east of
the Baboquivari Mountains.

CORRESPONDENTS: Elisabeth Kraemer (Bonn); Margot Hapgood,
Dorothy Bacon, Lesley Coleman (London); Susan Jonas, Lucy T.
Voulgaris (New York); Maria Vincenza Aloisi, Josephine du Brusle
(Paris); Ann Natanson (Rome). Valuable assistance was also
provided by: Carolyn T. Chubet, Miriam Hsia (New York); Earl
Zarbin (Phoenix); Marilyn Drago (Tucson).

For information about any Time-Life book, please write:
Reader Information
Time-Life Books
541 North Fairbanks Court
Chicago, Illinois 60611

Library of Congress Cataloguing in Publication Data
Abbey, Edward, 1927-
   Cactus country, by Edward Abbey and the editors of Time-Life
Books. New York, Time-Life Books [1973]
   184 p. illus. (part col.) 27 cm.
   (The American wilderness)
   Bibliography: p. 180.
   1. Natural history—Sonoran Desert.
   I. Time-Life Books.   II. Title.
QH88.A2   500.9'791'7   72-91599
ISBN 0-8094-1167-9
ISBN 0-8094-1169-5 lib. bdg.
ISBN 0-8094-1168-7 retail ed.

TIME-LIFE is a trademark of Time Incorporated U.S.A.

Contents

MILES

0 10 20 30 40 50

A Dry Corner of the Continent

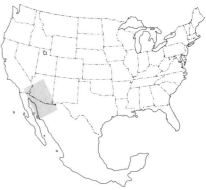

The arid wilderness explored in this book covers some 69,000 square miles of southern Arizona and northern Mexico (tinted rectangle above) and represents about half of the vast Sonoran Desert. The region, shown in tan on the detailed relief map at left, has a terrain both rugged and varied. Many mountain ranges break it up into broad plains and rough-sloped valleys. High peaks, indicated by black triangles, overlook jagged foothills with abandoned gold and silver mines and natural tanks—rocky depressions that conserve the spring rains for much of the year. The intermittent streams and gravelly dry washes, marked by broken blue lines, are the result of runoff from rare desert rains; they are found throughout the region, though they scarcely penetrate several great tracts of sandy wasteland, indicated on the map by red stippling.

Though harsh, and hostile to many plants, the region offers ideal conditions for the bizarre members of the water-storing cactus family, which thrive here in more than 140 species from pincushion cacti two inches tall to ponderous saguaros and cardons that reach heights of 50 feet and more.

1/ The Real Desert

None other than this long brown
land lays such a hold on the affections.

MARY AUSTIN/ *THE LAND OF LITTLE RAIN*

The real desert? Yes, but which one? I sit here on the terrace of this old stone house above Tucson in the foothills of Arizona's Santa Catalina Mountains and think about the deserts I have known. And the ones I've only imagined.

The city glitters softly, 10 miles down and away, under its tender veil of smog. Airplanes like fireflies circle slowly through the twilight. From this distance the city remains as inaudible as it is lovely. Moonrise over the Rincon Mountains, beyond a shore of clouds. Great gory sunset in the west, behind the jagged pinnacles of the Tucson Mountains. The clouds over that way, underlit by the sun, resemble boiled salmon—pink gold against the velvet purple sky. Such skies are common during the summer stormy season in the Southwest; I've seen them over the canyon lands of Utah, the burned iron hills of Death Valley, old lost adobe missions in Chihuahua, the white sands of New Mexico, the dunes of El Gran Desierto in northwestern Mexico. Which desert did I love the most?

Which lady did I love the most? I loved them all. But one was lovelier than any other. One was richer, more complicated, most various. For all its harshness, loneliness, cruelty and cunning, one desert haunted me like a vision of paradise. Still does, though now I live here. I mean that mountain-studded portion of southern Arizona and Mexican Sonora that geographers call the Sonoran Desert and botanists call the arboreal desert (because of the cactus, shrub and tree forests). Most people call it cactus country.

The Sonoran Desert by now has been divided, bisected and subdivided many times, not only by the cities of Phoenix, Tucson, Yuma, Nogales, Hermosillo, but also by an evergrowing complex of highways, superhighways, corporate factory farms, open-pit copper mines, power lines, dams, bombing and gunnery ranges and huge tracts of real estate. We must accommodate ourselves to the fact that the unspoiled desert no longer exists as a single integrated unit. The fragments that remain, however, comprise some of the most interesting wilderness areas on the North American continent.

I have looked into most of them and have a few things I want to say, beginning with the Superstition Mountains, working out from there to Organ Pipe Cactus National Monument and the peak and range of Baboquivari, going farther yet to the Kofa Mountains, and finishing up with two of the remotest and wildest areas left in the big cactus country, both south of the border in Mexico: the gulf coast of Sonora and the volcanic region called Pinacate.

I am not a naturalist; what I hope to evoke through words here is the way things *feel* on stormy desert afternoons, the exact shade of color in shadows on the warm rock, the brightness of October, the rust and silence and echoes of human history along dusty desert roads, the fragrance of burning mesquite, and a few other simple, ordinary, inexplicable things like that.

I saw the cactus country first in my student days, ranging out far from Albuquerque. Descending from the highlands of New Mexico and northern Arizona after 200 miles of nothing but grassland crawling with bald-faced cows and yellow pine forest creeping with smoke and fire, I glided into this new, unknown region of grotesque plant forms: bear grass in giant hummocks rearing from the rock; sotol, a 10-foot stalk rising from a nest of sawtooth leaves and topped with a plumelike cluster of creamy flowers; agave, the century plant, that floral monster, a 15-foot shaft surmounted by efflorescing blossoms of brassy gold, the structure based upon a rosette of swordlike blades with barbed edges and needle-tipped points. After that, descending still farther, I encountered varied cacti: cholla (in Spanish the word means head or skull), teddy bear, chain fruit, buckhorn, and cow's tongue prickly pear, clock-face prickly pear, Englemann's prickly pear. Then came the realm of the many-armed flame-flowered ocotillo, 10 to 20 feet high, looking something like a squid or octopus buried head downward in the sand; and fat leaning barrel cactus, fishhook cactus, pincushion cactus—empires of spine and thorn, needle and hair, hook and point and knife and dagger—to the crowning glory of America's Arizona rock garden, the saguaro cactus. Supreme symbol of the Southwest, the saguaro is a giant among cacti, a 20- to 50-foot-high fluted column of chlorophylled plant flesh that comes in as many different shapes and sizes as human beings do. Like planted people, no two alike, individual and idiosyncratic, each saguaro has its own form, its own character, its own personality. Or so it seemed to me then; and now, more than 25 years later, it still does. When nobody else is around, I talk to them. On simple subjects, of course.

Down from the hills, into the richest and liveliest of American deserts, a land dominated by the big cactus but home also of wild pigs called javelinas; reptiles like the coral snake, coon-tailed rattlesnake and Gila monster; eccentric arachnids—the scorpion, the centipede, the tarantula, the eight-eyed wolf spider. The big birds live here too: baldheaded redheaded turkey vultures, kin to the condor, king of all soaring things; hawks, in over a dozen varieties; golden eagles; the roadrunner, cousin to cuckoos. And little birds: the lively gray rock wren; the canyon wren, a sweet and lyrical singer; the cactus wren, builder of nests in the midst of cactus branches, a small bird with a big mouth and a song like the sound of a rusty adding machine. And others: ravens croaking in the stillness; tiny elf owls nesting in holes in the saguaro, great horned owls adorning telephone poles at night; the black crested *Phainopepla,* the only bird of its kind in the United States, whose name, translated, means glossy robe. There is a nice variety of mammals: mountain lion, bobcat, bighorn sheep, pronghorn antelope, mule deer and Mexican wanderers like the jaguar and wolf. The big cactus desert is blessed with many beasts, some venomous, some weird, but all—in their way—beautiful.

On that first trip, so long ago, I drove my old Chevy among the rocky hills and into the sunny southern reaches of Arizona through Tucson —still a small city then—and across the Papago Indian Reservation under a sapphire sky. I was bound for Organ Pipe Cactus National Monument, named for the tall plant that dominates the place. Why? Because it seemed about as remote a place as you could find.

Off in the distance, as everywhere in this desert land, rose the arid mountains, all rock and angles sparsely grown with brush, floating under cloud shadows, dappled with sunlight, colored by superstition and legend. I imagined them full of lost gold mines, sun-bleached skeletons of men and horses, antique rusty weapons, hidden springs, crumbling cabins, wandering trails, the abandoned hulks of mining machinery, 1922 Maxwells, gin bottles turning blue under the ferocious sun, all things old, worthless and wonderful.

I saw the Papago villages along the highway; stone and adobe huts, wooden ramadas for summer living in the shade, many children all brown as acorns, many horses, many goats, many cattle, many cannibalized automobiles resting upside down among the junk and garbage, chickens scratching in the bare, dusty yards. Occasionally I'd see a wagon, an old man under his sombrero on the seat and a team of horses, eight legs trudging along the highway, hauling hay, cattle feed, water, women, children, sometimes nothing. Over all, soaring without visible effort against the sky, drifted the hungry, arrogant, wide-winged buzzards, waiting for something somewhere soon to die. The patience and complacency of the scavenger, whose business never fails, whose customers always come.

Death and life usually appear close together, sometimes side by side, in the desert. Perhaps that is the secret of the desert's fascination: all lies naked, out in the open in this all too vulnerable land. Wherever we look we are reminded of death—by the glimmering wastes of alkali flats; by the burned-out volcanic hills; by a mesquite tree under a lethal burden of parasitic mistletoe, a plant as distinct from the Christmas sprig as stealing is from giving, delivering its kiss of death to the tree by means of suckerlike roots; by the occasional little white crosses along the roadways, marking the sites of fatal accidents on the heat-shimmering straightaways, by the remains of a maggot-swarming, dehydrated cow; by the hulk of a rotting saguaro, whose sloughing skin seems to present decay and decomposition in its most vivid form: nothing, not even the waiting vulture in the sky, looks more deathly than a dying giant cactus.

All, even these, are aspects of the desert: and with me it was love at first sight. Across the Papago Reservation I drove, across the solemn desert hills where the ranks and squads of saguaros towered over the rock, over the mesquite trees, over the bur sage and brittlebush. This was good saguaro country. They grew along the skyline of the hills, on the stony slopes, in the little meandering canyons creasing the hills, on the fans of rock debris that spread out toward the basins separating each range of mountains from the next.

I camped at night far out in the middle of the reservation, pulling off the main road and driving for maybe three or four miles into the desert on a winding wagon track. I built a fire of mesquite wood and cooked my supper in the evening gloom.

Autumn in the Sonoran Desert. The great horned owls lulled me to sleep, as I lay in my cheap Sears Roebuck amateur-outdoorsman sleeping bag in the middle of a sandy wash, across a cattle path. A flash flood could have washed me into the Gulf of California, but I didn't know any better. I slept well too, except that around midnight I was awakened by the distant sound of drumming and chanting. Off in the wasteland, out in the bush, some Papago were having a sing. The music came my way on small waves of wind, from a considerable distance, now here, now gone. I was not alarmed. Indians are no longer dangerous except occasionally when tooling their pickup trucks, loaded with sheep, wives and kids, down the asphalt trails.

I opened my eyes in the lavender twilight of dawn to see a tarantula, big as my hand (standard size) and furry brown as a muskrat, walking across the sand toward my face. Walking, I say, not crawling, not creeping; a tarantula stands up on its eight long black hairy legs and *walks* where it wants to go.

The tarantula's poison is not dangerous, the desert guidebooks assure us, despite its ancient reputation as an aggressive killer, and although the bite itself can be painful. Still, the tarantula looks much bigger than a spider should look, especially when viewed from ground level at a range of 30 inches. I rolled hastily aside, still zipped up in my Dacron sack, and watched him—her—it—walk on by in a straight line across the wash. Whatever the creature was hunting it was not me. Mostly the nearsighted tarantula eats insects and sometimes small lizards and mice. The tarantula in turn is the prey of a wasp known as the tarantula hawk. Also of cowboys with six-guns.

One time driving through western Texas I saw a car parked off the road and a group of tourists watching a tarantula stroll across the highway. I stopped to watch too. A moment later a pickup truck screeched to a halt close by and a large red-nosed man in cowboy costume rolled out and came up to us waving a revolver. "Stand back, folks," he said, "y'all stand back now." He aimed his piece at the tarantula and blasted away from a cautious range of six feet. One, two, three, four explosions, asphalt and gravel flying in all directions, before he succeeded in gunning down the terrified tarantula; on the fourth shot it vanished in a splatter of dust, lead, hair and fragmented chitinous tissue. "That there's a dangerous animal, folks," the cowboy said, lowering his weap-

Perhaps spurred by the mating urge, a male tarantula—usually a nocturnal prowler—takes a walk in the sun in the Sonoran Desert. These huge hairy spiders, with an average body length of two inches and legspans of five inches, are less menacing than they look. They bite only if teased, and their venom is not deadly to human beings.

on. What animal? We contemplated the bleared impact area on the edge of the pavement.

I don't fool with tarantulas myself. I drove on across the Papago Reservation to a fork in the road, with gas station, café and post office, called Why. Why, Arizona; named for the "Y" formed here by the junction. Ten miles down the road to the west lay the old mining town of Ajo (meaning garlic), occupied by the Phelps Dodge Corporation, site of one of the biggest open-pit copper mines in the world. A dirty smudge across the sky, waste from the plant smokestacks, provided plain evidence that the mill was in operation.

I took the south fork and soon reached the entrance to Organ Pipe Cactus National Monument. I didn't know it then but this was the place where I would later work for three winters as a seasonal ranger for the National Park Service.

More desert country; all about grew the gray-green shrub called creosote bush, most common of all low desert plants, with mesquite, paloverde and saguaro on the hillsides, and mountains, mountains, always more mountains in the background. And the vast quiet sky, with clouds and buzzards, as always. On the left, to the east, I could see the towering shape of Montezuma's Head, a 1,400-foot-high structure of volcanic materials, the sides as vertical as the walls of a building. But not unscalable, as I would learn one day, 20 years later.

I drove all the way to monument headquarters, 16 miles, without seeing a single organ pipe cactus. When I finally stopped I figured out why: all of the organ pipes grow on south-facing slopes; I had come from the north, not looking back.

The organ pipe cactus is a conspicuous plant, though perhaps not so impressive as the saguaro. At most the organ pipe grows to 10 or 15 feet, only about half the saguaro's height. Instead of a single main column the organ pipe, as the name implies, produces a cluster of branches from a single base. Though common in northwest Mexico, this cactus grows nowhere in the United States except in this part of Arizona, which is the primary reason the area was set aside by Presidential proclamation in 1937 as a national monument.

Near the sun-baked village of Lukeville, on the Mexican border, I turned west to follow a dirt road through the cactus "forest" to an oasis called Quitobaquito. On the way I saw my first Gila monster.

There it was, a fat, beaded bag of nonchalance, ambling across the road in front of me. I stopped the car and got out to inspect it, not getting too close, for this is one of the two lizards in North America with a venomous bite. (The other is a Mexican cousin.) My monster neither stopped nor turned but continued its leisurely crawl across the stony floor of the desert beside the road. I followed it with much more interest in it than it had in me. Finally, as my interest became too persistent, the big lizard took refuge under the low branches of a creosote bush. I squatted on my heels to study it for a while.

It was about 20 inches long, including the fat, heavy tail, and entirely enclosed in a scaly skin that resembled Indian beadwork, salmon and black. The legs seemed much too stubby for such a long and broad body, and in this respect the Gila monster reminded me of its distant kin the alligator. I poked it, gently, with a stick, and it whipped its massive head around and hissed at me; I had a glimpse of a pink-lined mouth and rows of small white teeth.

The Gila monster is supposedly quick and agile when seriously molested, but has no fangs and in any case its neck is so short that it cannot lunge and strike like a snake. The poison, secreted by glands in the mouth, is worked into the flesh of a victim by prolonged gripping and chewing. One of the legends concerning this lizard is that once it gets its teeth sunk in your flesh and the jaws clamped shut, it never lets go. I did not experiment. Another story has it that the Gila monster has no anus, and cannot eliminate wastes. False. Actually, the creature is defenseless against humans armed with anything more than their bare hands. Famous and hideous, protected by law as one of Arizona's natural tourist attractions, it nevertheless suffers much persecution from the ignorant, and may already be an endangered species.

Leaving the Gila monster in its natural habitat unharmed and only slightly alarmed, I went on with my journey through the dusty hinterlands of Organ Pipe. After a day and night at Quitobaquito, an uninhabited oasis of sweet, cool water and green cottonwood trees that I would come to know better some years later, I headed north, following a different road.

Somewhere out in the open desert of west central Organ Pipe I came to a fork in the road, with signboards. One sign said, "Park Hdqtrs 21 Mi"; the other something like "Primitive Road, Not Patrolled." Naturally I took the latter, which looked more interesting and led in the direction I wanted to go.

The old road took me through more miles of creosote flats, the creosote bush being the only plant of any size that grows in that wide arid basin between the desert mountain ranges. Jack rabbits in astonishing number sprang away from the road at my approach, seeming to swarm across the land like a plague of grasshoppers. Not enough coyotes to keep them in check.

As I rounded a knoll and headed down a long straightaway, five sleek pronghorn antelope leapt from the shade of some paloverde trees and raced along ahead of me, paralleling the road. I followed through the dust from 20 pounding hoofs, watching the white rumps bounce across the rough, brushy terrain. Glancing at the speedometer I clocked the pronghorns' pace at 26 miles per hour before they finally veered from the road and faded away into the flat, vast, dust-green emptiness of what the maps call Growler Valley. I thought of Africa. I thought of original America.

Another 40 miles of primitive road brought me to the town of Ajo and the highway. I headed the old Chevrolet homeward to Albuquerque through Gila Bend and Phoenix and what seemed like a thousand miles of cotton farms, feed lots, hayfields, used-car lots, power plants, housing plantations, barbed-wire fences and telephone lines—the fat rich commercial gut of Arizona.

The familiar dreariness did not dim my sense of the desert still waiting out there. I would not forget the rocky hills studded with giant cactus, the secret canyons winding into unknown places, the purple, shadowed mountains on the horizon, the rich complex of animal life, bird life, plant life, all that strange, sometimes bitter magic of the natural world. I knew that I would be back, many times.

NATURE WALK / To a Foothills Canyon

TEXT AND PHOTOGRAPHS BY DAVID CAVAGNARO

The time was April. I was visiting Edward Abbey for a few days, and I was also visiting the part of the Sonoran Desert he lives in and with, the ancient cactus and shrub desert of Arizona. Behind Ed's old stone house loom the steep, deeply eroded Santa Catalina Mountains; below lies a great sweeping plain through which the distant Santa Ritas and Tucson Mountains protrude like islands in a dry sea.

The desert's day shift was about to come on. The songs of wrens, flickers, doves and Gila woodpeckers mingled with the fading cries of coyotes; clouds of droning insects, emerged from their nighttime hiding places, surrounded blossoming mesquites. The sun peered over the eastern end of the Santa Catalinas, its low-angled rays gliding along the rugged range. Impatient to get out and explore, I downed a final cup of coffee, picked up my camera and struck off toward the forests of juniper and fir in the highlands.

My destination, one of the many deep canyons that cleave these hills, was only about three quarters of a mile from Ed's place. But as I headed toward it my pace slowed. The plain I was crossing—part of an enormous alluvial fan that extends for miles and miles—was fascinating in its own right.

Beneath my feet and all around me lay the eroded rubble of millennia, much of it carved from the mountains during wetter times produced by the distant breath of glaciers far to the north. The boulders and rocks and gravel have lent a wild, unsettled look to the landscape; time and again they have been washed across the skirt of alluvium by torrential floods that occasionally, even now, relieve the desert of drought.

This year, however, the winter rains had not come. The many washes, large and small, were dry. The huge saguaros that thrive in this rocky realm looked shrunken, their accordion pleats deeply folded because of the lack of moisture. Had the rains been right, vast carpets of verbena, owl clover and gold poppies would have been blooming on this April day. But here and there a stunted plant had blossomed quickly and set a few seeds. The rest, tough little capsules, lay dormant in the sand, waiting.

An unusual midwinter snowfall had brought a bit of moisture to the lower slopes of the Santa Catalinas. Wherever the meltwater had accumulated, flowers—zinnias, daisies,

A STAND OF SAGUAROS AT THE ENTRANCE TO AN ARROYO

penstemon—were now slightly taller and more numerous, and the graceful paloverdes were solid gold with blossoms. But on the higher, drier ground other paloverdes were bare of leaves, forced to rely entirely upon their green stems and branches for photosynthesis. Only a few blossoms testified to the life that persisted within these sturdy desert trees; they, too, like the dormant flower seeds, awaited rain.

On the large climatic scale of geologic time, the southwestern United States and northern Mexico are in the grip of a dry phase. Forests of pine and fir and the oak woods that fringe them have retreated to the tops of the highest, coolest mountains. Strange cacti, thorny shrubs and tough little desert annuals have advanced out of the southern desert highlands. For example, seedling saguaros will gain a foothold, over a period of years, a few yards farther up the rocky slopes of a range or progress a small distance farther north around its flanks.

But the expansion of the desert—or its contraction during a wet phase—takes place over a long period of time; in this larger climatic rhythm, a year is only a tiny vibration. And so there will be wet years and drought years for the paloverdes, saguaros and seed capsules I saw in this corner of the desert. For whatever hardships come, every living thing here is superbly prepared.

As I walked on, the sun's rays streamed down through the saguaro groves. Spiny pads of Engelmann's prickly-pear cactus, laden with buds and blooms in spite of the drought, were haloed by bright morning light, and the heat was strong and palpable; sunlight was reflected too from the brilliant silver leaves of the brittlebush. The dawn bird chorus had dwindled to periodic calls.

I settled for a while on a rock-strewn flat between two washes. Beneath a stone I found black darkling beetles, and a striped-tailed scorpion scurried nervously to and fro, disturbed by the sudden intrusion of sunlight. A species common in the Tucson area, this scorpion is a fierce predator, active at night: it uses leg-like pincers to catch insects, subduing them, if necessary, with a sting from its upturned tail. Although its

A STRIPED-TAILED SCORPION

sting is painful, the striped-tailed scorpion is harmless to man.

The ground was littered with old prickly-pear pads. The weather and the attacks of insects had reduced them to skeletons of woody lace. Some pads still bore a coat of masonry constructed by termites from mud and their own droppings. When the ground is moist, termites surface from subterranean passageways

ENGELMANN'S PRICKLY PEAR

and feed on fallen organic debris.

A tiny earthstar nearby, less than an inch across, was also a relic from the last rain. Mummified by the sun, its dry outer covering folded back against the ground, this strange relative of the puffball fungus contains a round central packet of microscopic spores that are eventually released into the wind.

The desert ground is a quiet place during the heat of the day, but close examination reveals a host of signs of nighttime activity. Within one small area I spotted the tracks of darkling beetles and Gambel's quail, a small pile of dry rabbit pellets, and a ring of seed chaff surrounding the nest entrance of harvester ants.

A black hole about three quarters of an inch wide and lined with spider webbing indicated the presence of a wolf spider somewhere deep within the cool recesses of the earth. These weird hairy spiders—with no fewer than eight eyes—emerge at night to hunt their prey on the move rather than trap them in a web. When mature, wolf spiders measure about two inches in leg span; in spite of their fearsome appearance, they are altogether harmless to humans, though their bite—inflicted only if they are provoked—is mildly toxic.

Shade at Noon

The morning was just about gone. The increasing oppressiveness of the heat finally drove me from the exposed plain in search of shade. I found it, not far from the deep canyon that was my ultimate goal, in the main arroyo that drains the canyon. Nurtured by abundant ground water,

TERMITE MUD ON A CACTUS PAD

AN EARTHSTAR PUFFBALL

A WOLF SPIDER'S BURROW

trees and shrubs grow larger in this gully, and their branches afforded welcome protection as I walked.

I soon found that I was not alone. From a honey mesquite directly over my head came a sudden explosion of feathers, and a white-winged dove settled several yards away in a paloverde and eyed me suspiciously. I had come upon it in nesting season, and it was instantly on guard. But I climbed up through the mesquite's stiff branches for a closer look at the nest. It was of simple design, a loose bowl of sticks set far out among the twigs, and within it were two elegant white eggs.

Other birds, too, had found haven in the dense growth of the arroyo. Gilded flickers and Gila woodpeckers flew in and out of holes they had carved high in the saguaros. I caught a brief glimpse of a cardinal among paloverde blossoms, and recurrently

A MOURNING DOVE (LEFT) AND ITS WHITE-WINGED KIN IN A PALOVERDE

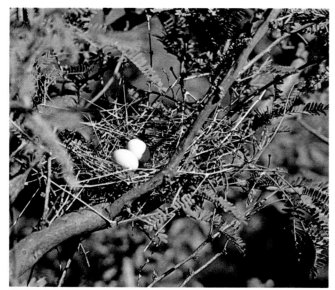

A WHITE-WINGED-DOVE NEST IN HONEY MESQUITE

A CACTUS WREN AND ITS NEST IN JUMPING CHOLLA

I heard the strange rasping call of the cactus wren.

The largest wren found in the United States, this spotted brown bird chooses the most densely armed cacti for nesting sites. Nearly every teddy bear, staghorn and jumping cholla in the area contained at least one nest, either old or freshly built. Each one was a neatly fashioned envelope of grass, tucked securely among the spiny joints of cholla, and each had a single, tube-shaped entrance hole.

A Good Place to Nest

The cactus wren is not the only bird that nests in cholla. The curve-billed thrasher is also a frequent occupant, and in one gnarled jumping cholla I found a mourning dove with two pinfeathered young. Relying upon protective coloration, adaptive stillness and the armor of the cactus itself, the dove allowed me to approach within two feet of the nest with no more reaction than the indifferent blink of an eye.

I paid a small price in exercising my curiosity, however, for as I stepped back from the nest my heel flipped up a loose joint of jumping cholla and it lodged firmly in the back of my calf. A few painful moments drove home the point that the dove had chosen its nest site wisely. The ground was littered with spiny cholla segments, some of which had taken root as new plants. The pendulous arms of the cactus were heavy with long strings of knobby green fruit, which may persist for many seasons—even years—before falling. Some of these would even-

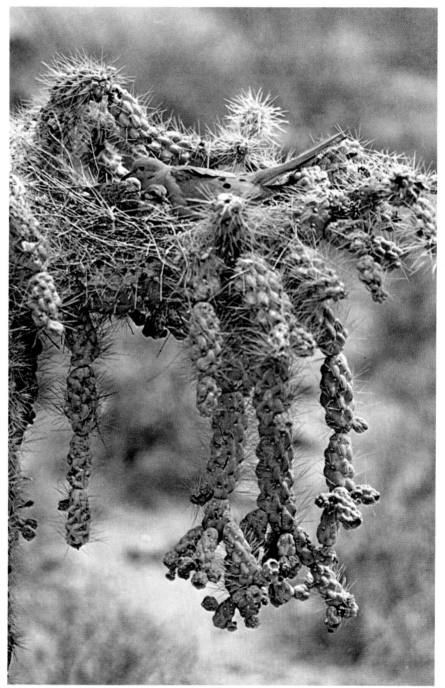

A MOURNING DOVE AND YOUNG IN JUMPING CHOLLA

tually generate new cactus plants.

Inspecting another cholla, this time with greater respect, I detected a jet-black cactus beetle hiding from the sun between the branches. A full inch in length, this peculiar insect, which feeds upon the succulent tissues of the cactus, belongs to the family of long-horned wood borers;

A CACTUS FLY ON BARREL CACTUS

A CACTUS BUG NYMPH

A CACTUS BEETLE

but it differs most markedly from nearly all its relatives in being entirely flightless.

What a strange landscape of enormous daggers this beetle inhabits; and yet, as I watched, it scrambled expertly among the spines, clinging firmly to them with sharp claws and strong legs, its tough exoskeleton immune to the pricking of the sharp points. And so this insect has penetrated perhaps the best line of defense in the desert. At the same time the spines help protect it from birds, rodents and skunks.

Another insect that has done well in a cactus habitat is the cactus bug, young nymphs of which I saw dotting the pads of Engelmann's prickly pear. Equipped with long, piercing mouthparts with which they suck

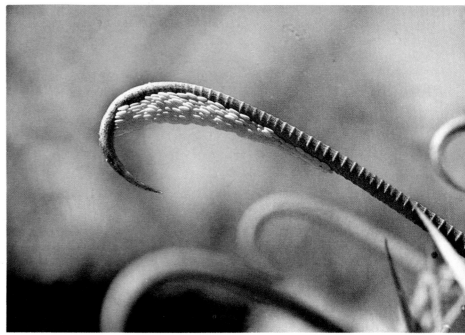

SYRPHID-FLY EGGS ON A BARREL CACTUS

plant juices, these insects, when numerous, may inflict quite noticeable wounds on the cactus pads.

An Army of Insects

Healthy cacti effectively fend off the hungry hordes of desert creatures that would relish their juicy flesh. But as soon as a plant is injured or dies of old age, a host of insects attack it. Along the arroyo bank was a fishhook barrel cactus, lately dislodged from its rocky perch. Though its tissues were still very much alive, tiny cactus flies were laying their eggs among the spines, and large syrphid flies hovered around it, droning incessantly in the midday heat, occasionally landing for a drink of exuding sap.

When I moved in for a closer look, I discovered that many of the long fishhook spines bore clusters of oval white eggs deposited by a species of syrphid fly. When the eggs hatch, the larvae of this insect burrow into the cactus, where they feed on the larvae of other insects.

Farther along the arroyo a pair of saguaros had died but had not yet fallen. Their flesh had long since been consumed by insects. Spines and slabs of dried skin lay at their base in a heap, home now for several funnel-web spiders. One 15-foot saguaro skeleton still stood erect, but the woody ribs of the other one arched like a sculpted fountain of water, bending toward the earth, to which their entire substance would eventually return.

As I walked on through the arroyo toward the mouth of the canyon, an early-afternoon breeze whispered

SAGUARO SKELETONS

A TARANTULA HAWK WASP

A DAINTY SULPHUR BUTTERFLY

A WILD HONEYBEE

A QUEEN BUTTERFLY

A SNOUT BUTTERFLY

A MARINE BLUE BUTTERFLY

along the dusty wash from the hot plain behind me.

Honeybees gathering pollen rummaged through the golden anthers of prickly-pear blossoms. Most of the gatherers seemed lazy with excess, but here and there I glimpsed a solitary bee flying the same mission with far greater speed. Green lynx spiders —predators that spin no webs—occupied some of the flowers, pouncing on the bees themselves or, more often, on small beetles, which are easier to catch.

In open places where the glare from white sand was intense, small silver clumps of wild zinnias attracted dainty sulphur and marine blue butterflies. They flitted from one blossom to another, sipping nectar while quaking in the breeze like tiny banners. I saw a few strange long-beaked snout butterflies land in twiggy bushes, and in their stillness they seemed suddenly transmuted into dead leaves.

The Butterflies' Colorful Warning

A large reddish queen butterfly, southern relative of the monarch, soared up the canyon on the breeze and settled near several scarlet lycid beetles among the puffy pale yellow acacia flowers. These net-winged beetles, like the queen and the monarch butterflies, are unpleasant tasting to predators, and they advertise the fact through their conspicuous coloration.

Enormous tarantula hawk wasps rattled slowly through the air on their way between acacias, their wings a brilliant orange blur against the sky. These wasps are nectar feeders themselves, but each female, in order to provide food for her larvae, must seek out and paralyze a tarantula with her powerful sting. She then finds an unoccupied underground burrow, drags in the helpless spider, lays a single egg upon it and seals the burrow entrance. When the egg hatches, the larva food is right there—in the form of a paralyzed tarantula. The female wasp may repeat the process many times before her own short life has ended.

Like the lycid beetle and queen

A BLISTER BEETLE

and monarch butterflies, the tarantula hawk's bright color warns potential predators. In this case, however, the warning does not concern unpleasant taste but potent sting. An animal that tangles once with this insect is not likely to try again.

In a thistle plant beneath the acacias, I saw another insect that predators may well beware because of its unpalatability: the orange blister beetle. Some species of this insect can also cause trouble for people; its secretions can cause nasty skin

A LYCID BEETLE ON CATCLAW ACACIA

sores. I watched from a prudent distance as several of these beetles probed the blossoms with long, strawlike mouthparts, sipping nectar from the thistle's tubular disk flowers. While some were feeding, others were mating and laying eggs underneath young buds. The eggs hatch just about as the buds open, and when a bee comes for pollen some of the larvae may manage to attach themselves to its hairs and be carried back to the bee's nest. Once the bee provisions and seals the cell in which it has laid its egg, the blister beetle larvae remain behind, destroy the egg and consume the carefully stored pollen themselves.

A Sound of Water

Beyond the acacias, the Santa Catalinas rise like a great convoluted wall. Ridges line the canyon I had come to explore, and as I entered it I heard the sound of falling water. It was only a trickle, a mere suggestion of the torrents that must pour from the mountains during a good storm. Now the flow was gentle, spilling over algae-draped rocks, slipping into quiet pools dotted with hundreds of tiny whirligig beetles and fringed with yellow monkey flowers —so called because the blossom resembles a monkey's face.

A stream on the canyon floor proved cool and refreshing, the sound of the water almost as much as its taste. As I drank, so did dozens of honeybees, butterflies and wasps, quenching their thirst along the wet sandy shore.

In this narrow stream-bottom oasis, broad-leaved trees largely re-

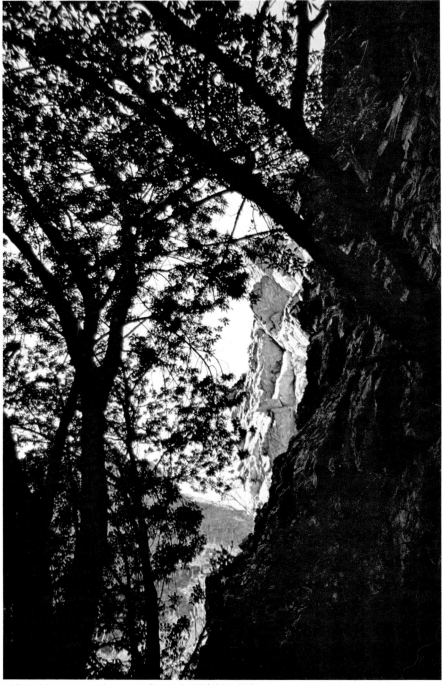

BROAD-LEAVED TREES FRAMING THE CANYON WALLS

place the desert trees and shrubs common in the arroyo below. The first trees I encountered were small, twisted western hackberries, whose dark green leaves nourish caterpillars of the snout butterfly. Farther along, I came to an ancient Arizona oak, the only one in the lower reaches of the canyon. The cool shade beneath its spreading canopy invited a rest from the afternoon heat.

But the oak also marked the end of easy walking for me. Above it, the canyon narrows and ascends more steeply. Vertical cliffs of weathered gray gneiss faced each other closely, casting the boulder-strewn cleft in shadow. Confined by this funnel of rock, the wind blew like a gale, roaring through the leaves of huge sycamore and Arizona walnut trees and rattling the slender daggers of sotol leaves as though a ritual dance

ASH LEAVES

were in progress. One of the desert's most beautiful lilies, the white-flowering sotol was once prized by the Pima Indians of this area for the strong fibers in its elongated leaves, which they used for weaving.

Here and there, as the sun slipped behind the west ridge, its last rays of light glowed upon a high rock face and illuminated the leaves of ash trees. Dusk had come early, and canyon tree frogs, a perfect color complement to the waterworn gneiss upon which they huddled, began to croak. Nearby, on a sheer face of rock, protected from above by an overhang and from below by a deep reflecting pool, a pair of black phoebes had built a half-cup mud and straw nest. As I watched, one of the birds returned from its insect hunting and settled to incubate the eggs.

There was activity, too, in a fallen

A SOTOL PLANT

A POOL AT THE CANYON MOUTH

sycamore log where honeybees had taken up residence. In the fading light bees flew home, one by one, entering through a hollow knot. The log hummed faintly as the workers ventilated the hive with their wings. Raccoon tracks in the soft sand and mud near the pool reminded me that soon the night creatures would be out and it would be time for dinner back at Ed Abbey's stone cabin.

I found a precarious route up a dry side gully and scrambled toward the crest of the ridge on the canyon's eastern flank. On the way I noticed that the harvester ants, having by now come out of the underground nests they occupy during the heat of the day, were foraging across the steep slope in search of seeds, their favorite food. A heap of spiny cactus joints was almost hidden in a

A LACY CACTUS SKELETON

crevice, dragged there from a nearby stand of teddy bear cholla by pack rats, which collect the cactus as a kind of barricade for their nests.

On the driest face of the ridge there were tiny woolly lipferns, growing where overhanging rocks protect them from the worst heat. It is an unlikely place for ferns, yet their fuzzy leaves and their ability

to remain dormant for long periods between rains enable them to survive where nearly all other ferns would quickly perish.

The wind faded to a breeze as I left the confinement of the canyon, perspiring from the exertion of my climb. Rewards come in strange packages, however; one little discovery made scaling the canyon wall seem especially worthwhile. As I neared the top of the east ridge I broke at last into the sun, warm now more from its yellow glow than from the heat of its rays. In a small rock crack I saw something bright and stopped for a close look.

A Spiny Carcass

Pinned between the rocks was a piece of lace less than an inch across, part of the shell of spines that once covered a fishhook pincushion cactus. The cactus had died and rotted away, leaving behind its more resistant spines like a miniature skeleton of white bones. In time they, too, would add their substance to the scarce soil accumulating slowly in this rocky place.

The sun was dipping toward the distant horizon. I descended an easy slope on the far side of the ridge and stepped once again onto the sweeping fan of alluvium that skirts the base of the range. The sun set behind tall saguaros, and the sky blazed. It was a warm evening. The wind had died entirely. The time had come for the daytime creatures to rest. I headed back for the cabin, hungry for dinner, no longer pausing to look and marvel, replete with the discoveries of the day.

WOOLLY LIPFERNS

A SUNSET OVER THE CANYON RIDGE

2/ The Mountains of Superstition

*The glittering treasure you are hunting for day
and night lies buried on the other side of that hill yonder.*

B. TRAVEN/ *THE TREASURE OF THE SIERRA MADRE*

One brutally hot day in mid-April my friend Douglas Peacock and I decided to go for a walk in the Superstition Mountains, a rugged but relatively accessible desert range some 30 miles east of Phoenix. It was too hot for hiking; we went anyhow, knowing the weather wasn't likely to cool off any for the next six months.

Driving north from Tucson to Florence Junction, then west halfway to Apache Junction, we reached a dirt road heading north over the desert through thickets of cholla and sparse stands of giant saguaro. Ten miles away through the haze loomed the rock ramparts of the Superstition Mountains. The western end of the range rises vertically from the desert floor, naked cliffs a thousand feet high surmounted by terraces, talus slopes, and farther, higher tiers of cliffs that merge with the main body of the range extending eastward toward the town of Globe. On the summit are boulder battlements, pinnacles, knobs and domes of bare rock, with a stubble of brush and trees here and there. A much eroded remnant of old volcanic structures, this range looks something like an antique Assyrian fortification, a mirage in the desert, a specter of olden times, abandoned by mankind.

Nobody seems to know the origin of the name Superstition for these mountains, but probably it is derived from the recurring, ineradicable, incurable belief held by so many over the past 150 years that somewhere in this giant rock pile lies an elusive treasure of gold—Apache gold, Spanish gold and, most elusive of all, the Lost Dutchman Mine.

We drove for five miles toward a pass in the mountains, bound for the end of the road and the Weaver's Needle trail head. Somewhere in the foothills, however, we missed a fork in the road and were soon stopped by a locked gate. A man was loafing nearby, apparently camped there, for we saw a pickup truck, tent and saddle horse with canvas water bags hung from the mesquite trees, their contents slowly evaporating—and thereby cooling—in the heat. The man wore a revolver strapped to his hip.

Characteristic of the area. The Superstition Mountains are full of gun-happy cranks, touchy old prospectors, truculent treasure hunters from faraway cities, all sorts of eccentric, unreliable freaks, misfits and oddballs attracted by the fame of the name of the place, coming here to live out their childhood fantasies of the Wild West. Little wonder that a few people get shot or mysteriously disappear from time to time in the Superstitions.

This particular gun nut was tolerably sociable, however; he lounged against the shady side of his truck looking tough and mean, but when we asked him to kindly direct us to the Weaver's Needle trail head he was willing to oblige. We got the information we needed and pulled out of there. I wasn't alarmed but Doug was annoyed: veteran of Vietnam, ex-Green Beret, he hates guns, hates gunfire, hates the mess a bullet makes in our all-too-vulnerable human flesh.

End of the road, head of the trail. We climbed out of the car and looked around. Bloody hot afternoon—the glare of the sun, the oppression of the heat became quickly apparent. Springtime in the Sonoran Desert. But the bees buzzing in the new-blooming mesquite and paloverde trees were happy. Big jojobas, large shrubs with tiny green leaves, grew among the cacti and trees; in season the jojoba bears a thin-shelled nut like an acorn, which it much resembles both in appearance and flavor. Some of the cactus was in bloom—the barrel with its purple blossom, the scarlet hedgehog and the brilliant yellow cups of the prickly pear.

Flowers; also garbage: we were only 40 miles from the great metropolitan miasma of Phoenix. Looking westward we could see, against the light, the 50-mile-wide pall across the sky. Is it possible that Phoenix may someday rise from her ashes? She lives in soot and smoke, dust and confusion and crime, half pickled in sulphuric acid, a city paying the price of gluttonous success.

Well, dammit, we were out to leave all that behind for a night and a

434443

couple of days. We stuffed our packs with supermarket dried foods, dehydrated spaghetti dinners, that sort of thing, plenty of jerky, chocolate, peanuts and cheese, and six quarts of water each; a heavy load but we knew we could need it. We might or might not find much free water in that burned-out wasteland behind yonder hills.

We started off.

The trail is dusty, steep, rocky and well beaten. Generations have trodden here, hoping to find an easy pot or two of that rare metal *Au*, hoping to reap, as Thoreau said, where they had never planted. Is not all gold fools' gold? And yet who can quite honestly completely resist the allure of hidden treasure? Not I. Not Douglas Peacock. Perhaps all truly good things come as gifts, unearned, unearnable. Or put the other way, anything you have to work, sweat and scrabble for is not worth having. Who knows? Ask the butterflies, flittering about among the barrel cactus, bright wings in the sunlight, free as leaves dancing on the wind. How many hours a day of honest labor do they put in?

We tramped upgrade through the sweltering heat, the pale glare of afternoon. Above us towered the walls of the main range, fretted on the summit with goblin rocks and hoodoo boulders. Nothing much alive was stirring except fools like us, and the ants and a few lizards here and there, dashing from shade to patch of shade, bush to rock and back; and of course, far up in the blue, a big soaring bird: cousin buzzard, indolent watcher of desert scenes.

In the shadows under the rock rattlesnakes watched us pass. We didn't always see them, but we knew that they were there, watching us. It was their kind of country.

What to do if a snake bit? In more than 25 years of wandering, mostly in the American Southwest, I have yet to be bitten by a rattlesnake nor has a companion been bitten. Not that I'm complaining.

God knows we've seen them often enough. Or not often enough. A couple of times, striding along in daydreaming euphoria, I have walked right over a sluggish, dozing rattler without seeing it—the friend behind has called my attention to what I almost stepped on. The point is that the rattlesnake cannot always be relied on to give the traditional audible warning; cold-blooded beasts, their body temperature determined by air temperature, they tend to be comatose, inert, when the air is too hot or too cold for them. Thus it is possible to get very close to a rattlesnake without rousing it, unless of course you are unlucky enough actually to step on it. That should always provoke the lightning strike.

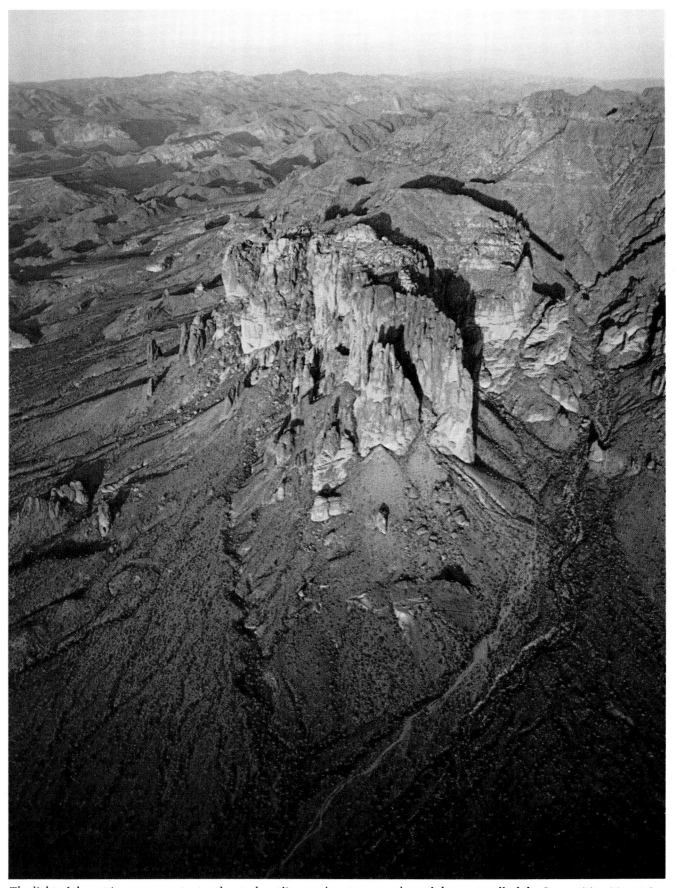

The light of the setting sun accentuates the stark outlines and austere grandeur of the west wall of the Superstition Mountains.

What then? I am no doctor, but having given it some thought and talked to a few experts, I feel free to advise:

First make sure it is a rattlesnake that got you. If it is possible—and not dangerous—kill the snake; your life or limb might depend upon proper identification. A victim can confuse the markings of harmless snakes, like the gopher snake, with those of a rattler. But one good look and a rattlesnake can seldom be mistaken for anything else: the spade-shaped head, typical of pit vipers, and the unique rattle on the tip of the tail make certain evidence. Since venom potency varies among different species of rattlesnake, treatment may require exact identification.

Anyway, you've established that it was a rattlesnake that bit you, you're sitting on a comfortable rock staring at the blood oozing from the fang marks on your calf, or forearm, let us say, and rolling a cigarette and deciding maybe it would have been better, after all, to have stayed at home this weekend, and you're wondering what to do, what to do.

Traditional first aid calls for the cut-and-suck treatment. Most desert hikers carry something like the Cutter snakebite kit, which includes a razor blade, a suction cup and a constriction band that acts as a tourniquet. A tourniquet, improperly applied, is more dangerous than most rattlesnakes and should rarely be used, according to current first-aid theory. The razor blade should be used only if you have a steady hand—or a friend has—and if you are more than an hour from professional medical help. In such cases incision and suction should be performed as quickly as possible. If the procedure is not started within five minutes of the snakebite, it is probably of little value. The recommended technique is to make a shallow incision, no more than an eighth of an inch deep and a quarter of an inch long, through each of the fang marks. Then apply suction over both cuts for at least 30 minutes to remove as much poison as possible before it is picked up by the bloodstream. Do not apply ice, and try to keep the bitten part immobilized. It is a good idea to eat or drink nothing until you get medical attention.

If your motor vehicle is close and a doctor is less than an hour away, you might best keep calm, place the constriction band above the bite to reduce blood circulation and head for help with all good speed. If you killed the snake, take it with you; the doctor will want to see it.

Exactly how dangerous is a rattlesnake bite? According to authorities on the subject, more than 8,000 people a year in the United States are bitten by rattlers; of these cases, fewer than 15 succumb. Chances of survival are excellent. I do not know from my own experience any cases in which death resulted from rattlesnake bite; I do know of one case in which a young man suffered an amputation because of a rattlesnake bite and lack of adequate and immediate first aid. Hiking alone in the Panamint Mountains west of Death Valley, he was bitten on the hand, attempted no first aid, walked for four hours back to his car and drove for three hours more to the nearest hospital. He lived, but lost an arm.

In the Sonoran Desert or big cactus country we have four major species of rattlesnake: the western diamondback, which is the largest (averaging five to six feet in length) though perhaps not the most potent; the tiger rattler, smaller but meaner; the blacktail rattler, rare; and the Mojave, or ringtail, rattler, which is common, wide-ranging and considered highly dangerous. We have as well several different varieties of sidewinder rattlesnake, much smaller and thereby generally less poisonous than the others. In neither size nor menace do we have rattlesnakes that can equal the magnificent seven-foot diamondbacks of such places as the swamps and hammocks of the Everglades.

This cursory review of rattlesnakes is not meant to exaggerate their danger to hikers and campers. In the first place, though common, they are easily avoided: all you have to do is watch where you put your hands and feet. And in the second place, even if you are foolish and careless enough to get bitten by a rattler, your chance of survival is in the area of 97 per cent.

Besides, though it won't ease the pain, remember that rattlesnakes, like all other living things in the natural world, fill a useful, perhaps essential, function in the stability of the ecosystem, helping for example to keep the population of rodents, their principal prey, within wholesome limits. This land is their land as well as ours; they were here before the Daughters of the American Revolution, before Coronado, even before the ancestors of Cochise and Geronimo made their way across the Bering Strait. They are elegant, cool, quiet creatures and quite simply, they *belong*.

So we tramped up Peralta Canyon, the creek bed dry and brittle as old bone, the rock and brush and trees all pale and dust-colored in the hot hazy light. A sycamore, a willow, a cottonwood—roots clutching the stone, searching out the last of the winter moisture. Looking for history, we took a brief side trip to a place called Geronimo's Cave, a shallow grotto under an overhanging bluff. But we found only bits and shards of Phoenix civilization, e.g., tinfoil, gum wrappers, aluminum cans, plastic sacks and Styrofoam baskets glittering in the sunlight.

Why keep carping about a little garbage? After all, we have to put it somewhere. Two hundred years of strenuous effort, hard work, sober sweat and careful planning went into this, grossest of all national products, to create on the North American continent the highest standard of consumption and the biggest pile of junk known to man or woman in all of human history.

Geronimo's Cave, this alcove in the rock littered with trash, has more mythic than historic significance. Here, according to legend, Apache warriors hid their gold, which modern-day treasure seekers, armed with revolvers and metal detectors, still scour the hills in hopes of finding. But there was never any treasure here except what the sun and the stillness, the desert breeze, the canyon pools, the birds and buzzards and barrel cactus have to offer.

A little beyond the cave, following the main trail, we came to Fremont Pass and our first view of fabled Weaver's Needle. Here if anywhere is the locus of the search for Superstition treasure, for here supposedly was the hideaway of Jacob Waltz the Dutchman and his hidden cache of gold.

Who was Waltz? Or Walz? Or Walts? The name has always had several spellings. And what is the Needle?

The latter can be said to resemble a needle only from certain points of view. Seen end-on, it does appear as a tall and slender spire, a dark pinnacle with perpendicular walls and a sloping, gently rounded summit. Seen from the sides, though, the Needle is longer than it is high. Rising 1,500 feet, it is made entirely of volcanic rock, mostly basalt, and according to geologists is actually the eroded remnant of a volcanic neck or plug—solidified magma that once closed the throat of a dead volcano. The original volcano having long since been completely eroded out of existence, the more resistant igneous material still remains.

The slender spire known as Weaver's Needle (center) has long served as a beacon for treasure hunters in the Superstition Mountains. According to local legend, it is supposed to have been named by a dying prospector as a principal clue to the location of precious deposits of gold ore.

Jacob Waltz the Dutchman, really a German, from Deutschland, apparently arrived in the Phoenix area around 1862 and died there in 1891. These dates have been well established, supported by still existing newspaper records. During the 30 years he lived in the Phoenix area the Dutchman achieved local fame by disappearing eastward from time to time, in the direction of the Superstition Mountains, and coming back with his saddlebags full of gold. According to the legend Waltz cashed in, over the years, some $254,000 worth of gold ore, a fantastic sum of money for that period. According to available evidence, however, as spelled out by journalist Curt Gentry in his book *The Killer Mountains,* there is no proof that Waltz ever sold more than $20,000 worth—a much more likely figure. All that is known for certain is that Waltz had found a little gold somewhere—where, no one knows. So it remains quite possible that the Dutchman's mine never existed at all except as fantasy in the minds of generations of treasure seekers—although mere lack of evidence was never enough and never will be enough to shake the faith of the devout. As with the devotees of any other cult, the more improbable the story the more tenacious is the gold seekers' belief.

The connection between the Needle and the Lost Dutchman Mine is this: as in most lost-gold tales, Waltz waited until his dying hour to reveal the location of his mine. In delirium on his deathbed, according to Gentry, he told his mistress, one Julia Thomas, and a boy named Reiney, "There's a great stone face looking up at my mine. If you pass three red hills you've gone too far. The rays of the setting sun shine on my gold. Climb above the mine and you can see Weaver's Needle."

Thus Julia Thomas became the first of many to spend her final years in a fruitless search for the Dutchman's Mine. For nearly a century since Waltz's death hundreds of people, possibly thousands, have tramped around in the bleak and barren hills trying to make sense of a dead man's elusive clues. Weaver's Needle, a striking landmark in itself, has quite naturally been the focal point of these many expeditions. The hills are pocked with prospect holes and littered with abandoned campsites, spent cartridge shells and—they say—missing persons.

Quite naturally this most famous of lost-gold-mine legends has attracted crackpots, treasure fanatics and easy-money freaks from all over the country. Most of them, venturing for the first time into desert mountains, overawed by the tradition of rattlesnakes, ghosts, Apache warriors and outlaw gunslingers, come stumbling in here with revolver strapped to nervous paleskin hip, with high-powered scope-sighted rifle slung on palsied shoulder. It's worse than opening day of deer season. No wonder there have been at least 36 verified deaths and disappearances in the area (according to Gentry) since that old joker Waltz croaked out his final words in a sleazy pad on skid row in Phoenix.

One final twist: the geologists assure us that gold will never be found in the Superstitions, unless it was carried here from somewhere else and cached. These contorted hills are composed mostly of igneous materials such as tuff and andesite—the lava and ashes of ancient volcanic convulsions—that are rarely if ever found in the presence of gold. Chemically impossible. Gold is where you find it? No doubt. But you won't find it here, the experts say.

Well, Douglas and I found no gold, no human skeletons in picturesque disarray, but we did see, although it had been a dry winter, a few spring flowers. Near Piper's Spring below Weaver's Needle we came upon the flamboyant little orange blooms of globe mallow, woolly golden desert marigold, violet phacelia and the delicate, slender blue flower with the name of bluedick. These are annuals that can grow anywhere in the desert when moisture conditions are favorable. In good years they may cover entire hillsides with masses of color.

But Piper's Spring was dry that season. Good thing we had plenty of water in our packs. We left the trail and wandered down the dry stream bed of what the maps call Boulder Canyon, below the Needle. There was not the slightest trace of water anywhere on the surface of the canyon floor. We kept going, shuffling through the arid sand, picking a way among and over the boulders. The canyon sank into bedrock, forming a narrow gorge, and here we discovered a series of lovely natural tanks in the solid rock—holes drilled in the stream bed by pebble power during eons of flash floods. Some of the holes were partly filled with month-old water from the most recent rain.

We stopped to admire. Douglas went for a dip in the biggest of the potholes, waist deep. Although the water in the pools was old and stagnant, much condensed from long evaporation, it still contained plentiful aquatic life. Tadpoles, mosquito larvae, and water bugs known locally as "boatmen" swam indolently about among the soft green strands of algae. A microscope would certainly have revealed a far denser world.

Some of the smaller pools contained no life at all that was visible to the unaided eye. In these isolated aquaria the processes of reproduction and decomposition, aggravated by water loss through evaporation, had terminated in a micro-habitat hostile to life. The metabolism of the little community had passed through the anabolic into the catabolic phase—that is, from growth to overgrowth and death. Total catastrophe for this miniature world within worlds: the banquet of life became a feast of fools, a teeming culture bouillon, then finally a quiet little disaster area picked over by transparent scavengers from the bacterial realm, swarming through the clear but toxic soup.

Merely an episode, of course, in the endless biodrama of a peaceful desert hidden place. The next flood to come down the canyon would flush the pools of their poisonous residue and refill them with fresh material and a reinvigorated medium, providing new opportunities, new catastrophes, ever-new returns.

Twilight filled the canyon, saturated the clear air in which we, like the smaller creatures in their fluid spheres, stirred ourselves. The sky became rosy, the silent evening took on a lavender tint, the storm-carved basaltic rock, scoured and polished by 10,000 roaring floods, changed in tone from sober gray to a somber, surrealistic purple blue.

We made camp on a long slick rock ledge beside one of the longest and clearest of the pools. We built a little squaw fire of mesquite and cooked our supper: beef stroganoff out of a box from a Tucson supermarket; cocoa and cookies for dessert. Among the rocks above our campsite we found a deposit of cartridge brass: .38s, .44s, .45s, .30-30s, .22s. Who had been potting whom from here and why?

Old Weaver's Needle rose against the evening sky, wrinkled with wear, wrapped in shadows, resting on its pedestal of stratified volcanic tuff, surrounded by clusters of goblin rocks—dumbbells, gargoyles, drunken soldiers, porphyritic phalluses, pregnant goddesses, Easter Island stone faces, petrified tyrannosaurs.

Javelina sign—tracks and droppings—around the waterholes indicated that these animals had stopped there recently. Also coyote, skunk and badger; we could probably expect a few visitors sometime during the night. We heard a canyon wren, a thrasher, a flock of quail somewhere out in the cactus and creosote brush.

Douglas banked our fire with sand, not to put it out but to make charcoal. In the morning we would use the charcoal to filter the pothole water, trying to purify it, since we had used most of the canteen water we had packed in. Nevertheless, on the next day, despite our precautions, we both got slightly ill on the long trek around the Needle on the eastern side. From the water? Perhaps; perhaps we hadn't purified it enough. Or maybe it was the heat. Or then again, as legend would have it, maybe it was a bit of the Dutchman's Curse.

Nobody gets in and out of the Superstition Mountains *completely* untouched. Even the most hexproof infidels cannot escape the power of such a magic name, the glamor of that sinister reputation, the occult touch of all those bored and restless haunts, the spirits of the place.

The Anatomy of a Colossus

PHOTOGRAPHS BY WOLF VON DEM BUSSCHE

Although it is the mightiest of all of Arizona's desert plants, the saguaro has no secret weapon or unique armament with which to combat the drought and heat of its environment. Less formidable members of the cactus family also employ its protective mechanisms, some of which are shown on the following pages in pictures taken at the Saguaro National Monument near Tucson. What sets the saguaro apart from other cacti is its sheer size, and everything else about it is correspondingly spectacular in scale.

The saguaro's root system, shallow but spread wide to absorb maximum rainfall in the thin, quick-draining desert soil, may cover an area as big as 100 feet in diameter. Aided by an expansible, bellowslike skin, the saguaro may increase its girth by 50 per cent or more as its spongy interior sops up one summer's rainfall. After a relatively wet desert summer, a large saguaro may weigh as much as seven tons, of which water constitutes 75 per cent or more. By making only sparing use of its stored-up moisture, a plant can live for a year or two without another drop of rain.

In the course of a century of bearing fruit, a mature saguaro may produce as many as 40 million seeds. But only three or four seeds out of that total produce plants that survive to maturity, according to one botanist's estimate. This high mortality rate is due both to the general hardships of survival in the desert and the particular passion of white-winged doves, ground squirrels, coyotes and other creatures for the saguaro's sweet, succulent fruit.

Even under conditions ideal for the species, the saguaro's growth rate is ponderously slow. A seedling that does survive usually takes nine years to grow six inches tall, and a plant that reaches the age of 40 will be no more than eight to 10 feet tall. Yet a number of saguaros have lived to roughly 200 years, and attained a height of 50 feet—the height of a five-story building.

To the nonscientist, standing in a saguaro forest, statistics matter less than the sense of awe that engulfs him in the presence of these splendid desert colossi. Puny as he feels, however, he can enjoy a stir of pride as well. For the saguaros grow nowhere else on earth other than the Sonoran Desert. They are, as the naturalist Paul Griswold Howes has put it, "something purely and wonderfully American."

Having defied the astronomical odds against its survival, this saguaro has reached the stage of magnificent maturity—over 130 years old and 30 feet tall. Its branches emerge about one third of the way up its trunk.

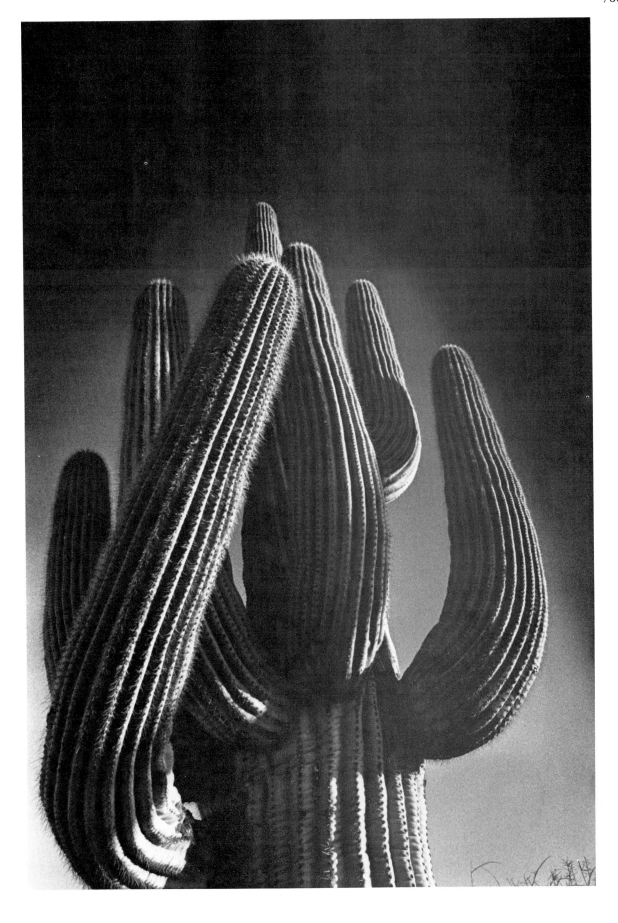

A mere adolescent, probably between 40 and 50 years old and about 13 feet tall, this saguaro betrays its immaturity by its branchlessness. The slow-growing species rarely produces arms before the age of 75, and a saguaro growing in a poor site may remain branchless throughout its long life.

Cottonlike blobs and supple spines identify a youthful saguaro or recent growth on an older plant. The blobs, which dry as the tissue beneath matures, provide shade for the soft young skin. The spines, which stiffen with age, ward off would-be nibblers and help temper desiccating winds.

This majestic saguaro, probably 150 years old, shows its age in several ways. It soars nearly 35 feet from a base about two feet in diameter —dimensions rare in plants less than 130 years old. Its glistening skin, whose waxy surface reduces moisture loss through evaporation, is mottled with brown, and many spines on its lower trunk have atrophied and fallen off.

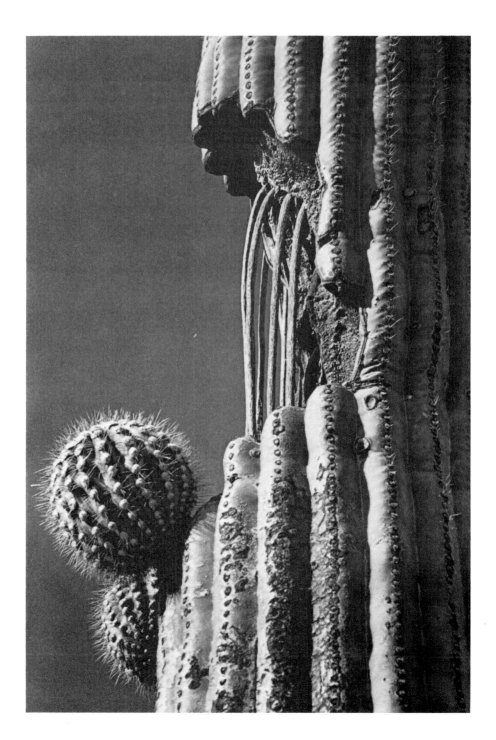

A long-dead saguaro (left) has dwindled to a skeleton of woody ribs, with the pith that once filled its rib cage now reduced to a dried-out pile. Saguaro trunks have eight to 15 ribs, depending on the individual plant's age and size. The ribs, strong enough to dull a knife blade yet flexible as whalebone, also provide a skeletal structure for both trunk and arms.

A wide gash in a saguaro's trunk reveals the thickness of the expansible water-storing tissue that lies between the plant's skin and its supporting ribs. The two knobs below the wound are budding branches whose growth may have been triggered by the injury itself.

A saguaro forest covers a bajada, or rocky slope. The giant cacti grow best on such slopes; rugged hills above provide them with the runoff of infrequent rains and protect them from strong winds. As the slope levels out (background), the saguaros give way to ironwood and mesquite, plants better adapted to the drier, sandier flats.

3/ Winters in Organ Pipe

The desert...is made like an old-fashioned museum. Each object is an individual specimen, standing on its own solitary pedestal. WILLIAM T. HORNADAY/ *CAMPFIRES ON DESERT AND LAVA*

A man or woman could hardly ask for a better way to make a living than as a seasonal ranger or naturalist for the National Park Service. The pay is modest but the atmosphere is good. Some of the routine might become irksome but the scenery is always nicely assembled. In what other occupation can you be paid an honest wage for doing what most people would regard as a vacation? The boss is usually far away in Washington and your companions are usually amiable; there's something about the Park Service that attracts good men and women.

True, you have to wear a semimilitary uniform and keep your hair trimmed back; but this indignity is a small sacrifice in return for all the fresh air you can breathe, more stars than you can count, more constellations than you can learn to name, more bugs and bees and bears and birds and bats than you can find in any field guide yet written.

Finally, there is this to be said for seasonal work of any kind. Whenever the hours tend to drag, the customers become tiresome, you have that most wonderful event of all to look forward to and comfort yourself with: termination day. End of the season. Out of work again at last and free to starve or thrive, as you make it, in your own style.

What I started to say is that back in 1968 I was offered a job as a seasonal park ranger at Organ Pipe Cactus National Monument. Organ Pipe, or ORPI for short, is a unit of our national park system, an area of some 516 square miles of desert and desert mountains on the Mexican border beginning 100 miles west of Tucson. Square in the middle of the Sonoran Desert, Organ Pipe has a tourist season that begins in November and ends in May, the remainder of the year being much too hot for pleasure. Only the most dedicated of desert aficionados venture forth during the 95°-to-105° days of June, July and August.

My job began in early December and ended in the middle of April. I lived in the south half of an old military Quonset hut, vintage World War II, that had been relocated there in the early development days of this park. The north half of the hut was occupied by Bill Hoy, ranger-naturalist and desert rat first class. I spent one or two working days each week tending the public campground, and that was the least interesting part of my job. In this role, wearing my sharpest Smokey Bear suit, I greeted the camping public, collected fees, kept records and collated statistics, provided elementary guide service and occasional first aid—and kidnapped rattlesnakes.

Campgrounds and garbage cans attract birds and rodents; birds and rodents attract snakes. Part of our educational task was trying to encourage people to accept snakes as natural and useful inhabitants of the desert, not as monsters to be murdered on sight. Most of this went over well. Given half a chance park visitors are eager to learn what they can about a new environment. But many still balk and boggle at venomous reptiles, especially the noble rattlesnake. When a rattlesnake was spotted in the campground, therefore, it became necessary, for the rattlesnake's own good as well as that of the campers, to capture it alive and relocate it. For this purpose we used a tonglike instrument three and a half feet long, designed for picking up scraps of paper and other litter, but also handy for snatching snakes without harming them.

Holding the rattler in this gadget's firm but gentle grasp I would dump it in a garbage can, put the can in the back of a pickup truck and transport the snake out into the desert to the recommended minimum of five miles from the campground. There, always at the same site, I would stuff the rattlesnake down a gopher hole, always the same hole. (This was my own idea.) Over the course of three winter seasons I placed at least a couple of dozen in that one little hole, trying to create a true snake pit. They wouldn't stay.

Campground duty out of the way, the primary job was patrol. On foot and by four-wheel-drive vehicle I had the privilege of wandering the trails and back roads of desert, mountain and borderlands, all within the boundaries of Organ Pipe—a big place.

A grand place. Around 8 in the morning I'd saddle up the old government truck and set forth into the outback, following my assigned route for the day. No one could possibly patrol the entire park in a single day or even in a week; therefore the patrols were worked out in advance and fitted to a schedule in such a way that over the course of a month most of the park would come under observation at least once.

The procedure required so much time because I was the only full-time patrol ranger. The job fell to my lot because I was relatively inexperienced, not very bright, wore my sideburns long and was only a seasonal, not a career, man. The career men—the regulars—had to stick around headquarters and do the professional work: repair traffic counters, sell postcards, fill out report forms, answer the telephone. I exaggerate and oversimplify—but not by much.

One patrol might cover what is called the Puerto Blanco Drive. This is a 51-mile loop road that begins near park headquarters, close to the highway, and winds over the hills and across the flats of the western side of the park.

Winter mornings I liked, the sunlight slanting in from the southeast, long shadows over the rock and brush and sand—a cool, crisp and vivid world. The road I followed is rough, dusty, rocky, with tight curves and sudden deep descents into gullies radiating from the base of the mountains. Along these watercourses, always dry except after summer storms, grow the predominant trees of this desert: ironwood, mesquite, two varieties of paloverde. All are legumes, a family that includes the pea clan; none grow more than 20 feet tall, all have tiny leaves, thorny branches and look more like big shrubs than conventional trees.

Ironwood, as the name says, is an exceedingly hard and heavy wood. The core of it will blunt the edge of ax or saw, and a solid chunk will sink in water. Yet the wood when dead is very brittle and breaks easily against a rock or another ironwood branch. As fuel, especially for campfire cooking, it is unexcelled, burning slowly, smokelessly and very hot. There is no better way to broil a piece of meat than by laying it directly upon a bed of ironwood coals. South of the border in the state of Sonora, ironwood is much in demand as a household fuel and may soon disappear from the Mexican deserts. Year by year the professional woodcutters fan out ever farther across the land, hacking and hewing to supply the needs of the rapidly growing population. They too wish to eat, live and multiply, these woodcutters, and so the ironwood and after it the mesquite will have to go. Mexico is already in the swarming stage, that busy time that precedes destruction.

At a certain high point about three miles from headquarters I would stop to admire the morning sunlight on Pinkley Peak, a multicolored chocolate-vanilla-strawberry mass of compacted volcanic rocks standing more than 3,000 feet above sea level. Through field glasses, I would survey the mountainside for desert bighorn sheep, feral burro or—quite rare in this particular area—white-tailed deer or desert mule deer.

To the north is an almost level alluvial plain dominated by creosote bushes, with the dark green of mesquite, the pale yellow green of paloverde and the gray green of ironwood along the sandy washes. Nobody lives out there now, although someone did once; the ruins of a 1920s homestead still stand in a cleared patch of land near the northern boundary of the monument.

On the east the Ajo Range, on the west Kino Peak and the Growler Mountains wall in this valley. Twenty miles to the north I could usually see a thick plume of poisonous smoke rising from the stacks of the Ajo copper smelter, compliments of the Phelps Dodge Corporation. Coming up from behind a conical desert hill, it created the effect of a smoking volcano. When the wind was northerly, however, this banner of industry could not be seen, because then the smoke and sulphuric wastes were diffused through the air of Organ Pipe itself, obscuring the view in all directions.

My second favorite stop along the Puerto Blanco patrol was at a place called Redtail Well. Taking a dim jeep trail that is closed to visitors, I would come after half a mile to the scattered remains of a miner's shack. Here were and maybe still are some rusted buckets and shovels, a midden heap of bean and sardine cans, and a hand-dug well. The well when I first found it was loosely covered with a few splintery boards; from the depths arose the unmistakable stench of decomposing meat. Taking my flashlight I peered down through the fumes into the well and saw a dim yellowish shape, too big to be a jack rabbit, maybe a bobcat, maybe a coyote, floating just below the surface of the oily water 20 feet below.

Hard to believe that an animal as agile as a cat or as intelligent as a coyote could have fallen into a well, no matter how desperately thirsty it might have been. The puzzle intrigued me for a while; finally I concluded that someone had shot the animal and dumped it in the well to hide it from the suspicious eyes of park rangers.

The smell of the decaying beast lingered around Redtail Well for the best part of my first winter season. Week by week I watched the remains slowly dissolve and disintegrate. Submersion in water retarded the natural process; had the animal been on the desert it would have been eaten up, dried out and rendered thoroughly clean and innocuous in a much shorter time.

A year later the corpse had disappeared, except for a few furry fragments. I nailed the boards together with cross members and weighted the cover with rocks, hoping to prevent another accident. If it was an accident. I didn't want to have to investigate smells again and find a jackass, a cow or a tourist down in there next time, presenting us with the forlorn sight, as Faulkner wrote in the novel *Mosquitoes,* of "that mute inopportune implacability of the drowned."

The jeep trail goes beyond Redtail Well to a natural basin in the rock called Redtail Tank; from there it forks, one road dead-ending at a copper mine deep in the hills, the other meandering on down a rough solid-rock gulch toward a place called Senita Basin, near the other end of the Puerto Blanco loop. In that area can be found a group of small abandoned gold and silver mines, including one known as Lost Cabin Mine.

The old copper mine, I've forgotten its name, was not so much a mine as a "diggings"—a prospect tunnel. It lay at the terminus of a two-mile hand-built road. I always walked the two miles, and it was a fine walk. Ocotillos 15 feet tall grew along the way; in March and April each spiderlike branch would be tipped with a scarlet cone of tiny flowers, looking from a distance like flames. Neither tree nor cactus, the ocotillo occupies a genus—*Fouquieria*—all its own. After each rain these plants take on a sheath of green leaves and do some hasty growing while the moisture lasts. When the inevitable drought returns, usually within a week, the leaves drop off, and growth is halted for a while until the next rain.

At times, walking that road, I'd hear a ghastly, spectral cough coming from above, as if out of the sky. A single powerful cough, like a giant clearing its throat. I could not imagine what it was, for looking up I would see nothing, no raven, no vulture, nothing in the air. Another mighty cough. I look again, my glance guided this time by the sound of clattering rocks on the hillside above, and see a shaggy little feral burro, ears up like semaphores, looking down at me. This burro is a footloose descendant of domestic burros lost or freed generations ago by pioneer miners. The cough is a warning sign, an alarm, a threat: I have invaded its territory. But I am no more willing to be intimidated than the burro; I walk on.

The feral burros are not exactly a blessing in the Southwest. Some biologists think that the burro is multiplying too fast and encroaching on the habitat of the bighorn sheep, consuming much of the latter's forage. The question at this time has not been definitely settled, but a program has been launched to capture and remove all the burros at Grand Canyon, where the competition between burro and bighorn is severe. A similar program was undertaken at Organ Pipe in 1978. The bighorn sheep was there first—thus the usual argument. But if the burro is better adapted to survive in desert areas, why not let it? An interesting issue. Perhaps the answer is that we need more predators, especially mountain lions, for whom the burro would be an easy prey. Or perhaps we should make the burro an official big-game animal, so that every trophy hunter can have the head of a jackass mounted on his rumpus-room wall.

Back on the Puerto Blanco road, the patrol continued to what is called Dripping Springs, one of the only two major natural and permanent water sources in Organ Pipe. At the end of a spur road I'd park the truck and take a short walk up a switchback trail to a shallow cave on the hillside. There in that cool little grotto was the spring, delphic, oracular, a deep oval pond under a dripping dome of rock. A small stream runs from the spring between succulent banks of watercress, purple asters and scarlet penstemon, dropping from there down into a rocky, brushy ravine where all of the surplus water is soon taken up by plant life or lost again underground. In the basin of the spring, swarms of mosquito larvae wriggle through the water; a few drowned honeybees float on the surface, others gather at the edge sipping up moisture. The water has a milky coloring, probably from minerals leached out of the rocks, but it always tasted clean and sweet to me.

The footpath beyond the spring leads to the saddle of a ridge, a big notch of rock with high walls of buff-colored volcanic rock on either side. This is the Puerto Blanco itself—the white gateway. From this high point you can look south over the granite hills and old mines of Senita Basin, far across the border to the jagged mountains of Sonora.

Toward the southeast the ridge rises gradually to the summit of Pinkley Peak. I climbed that mountain several times during my tour of duty at Organ Pipe, partly for the fun of it, officially to take rain gauge measurements. Once I found the dried-out hulk of a brown pelican close to the mountain's highest point. What was a pelican doing up there? No one knows. Blown astray, maybe, by the winds of a Gulf storm.

A few more miles of lovely primitive country, and the road leads past an old well, windmill, corral and line cabin. Used by rancher Henry Gray when I was working there, the corral had a trap gate that could

As majestic as the 16th Century Aztec Emperor for whom it was named, the towering butte called Montezuma's Head (center) dominates the landscape in the northeastern part of Organ Pipe Cactus National Monument. In this panorama, the 3,634-foot-high mountain, formed of various kinds of volcanic rock, resembles the upper half of a hulking giant seen from the rear. The "head" itself is a monolithic block of rhyolite, a granite-like type of lava.

be rigged to open inward but not outward. Since the trough inside the corral held the only water for miles around, it made good and sufficient bait for catching cattle and horses. The old cabin across the road was used for storage and as a bunkhouse before the days of pickup trucks, when a ride of 30 miles on horseback or by team and wagon might take a whole day. A hitching rack, a table and a bench stood beside the cabin, under the welcome shade of a big mesquite tree.

Cattle grazing was once a major problem at Organ Pipe. Long before the area was designated a national monument in 1937, the Gray family had begun cattle operations here. Although they acquired title to only 157 acres, their long occupancy and use of the land gave them powerful squatter's rights, which the Park Service was bound by law and custom to respect. Year after year several hundred head of scrubby cattle ranged the hills and plains of Organ Pipe, trampling the seedling cacti, stripping the soil of its natural cover, browsing on the mesquite and ironwood, and polluting the water holes with dung and parasites. Special appropriation bills were introduced in Congress to buy out the Gray family, but none of them were passed. It was only after Henry Gray and his brother Robert died in 1976 that the grazing issue was resolved and the remaining stock removed.

Even at that, it appears unlikely that Organ Pipe will ever be completely rid of cattle. Like corrals, cowboys and horses, the cattle business has endured as a fundamental part of the American West for a century. Ranching still goes on just outside the north and east boundaries, and stray cows are to be expected. The same is true along the south boundary, where Mexican herds graze: here the fence is frequently cut by drug smugglers.

For my part, if the only choice at Organ Pipe were between overgrazing by cattle or more asphalt trails for motorized tourists, I would prefer the cows. Fortunately that choice doesn't have to be made. Most of the monument has been set aside as permanent wilderness, wide open to any and all with interest enough to leave the security of their cars and try the will of their legs and feet and hearts.

Cattle grazing rates as merely a small misfortune at Organ Pipe when compared with the catastrophe copper mining would be. America's national monuments are supposed to be left undisturbed by commercial enterprise, but during the Second World War, under the guise of military necessity, several desert areas, among them Death Valley and Organ Pipe, were made available for mineral exploration. This was supposed to have been just a temporary measure, but it was not repealed by

Congress until almost 35 years later. During this period there were scores of eager prospectors swarming through the area, staking out several thousand mining claims. Although there was no mining going on at Organ Pipe in the early 1980s, and in spite of the fact that the government has invalidated all of the recorded claims that were filed previously, the damage has already been done. In their wake, the mine operators left the landscape cluttered with spoil piles, litter and dangerous shafts.

On with our Puerto Blanco patrol: After the corral-windmill-cowboy cabin come miles of open desert. I pass a cristate saguaro, so called for the tumorlike cross-shaped growth of tissue on the crown. Here too grows the Mexican jumping-bean bush, many of them, with reddish leaves, skin-burning sap and the autumn fruit that, when bored into by a moth larva, becomes the well-known jumping bean; its motion is caused by movements of the worm inside. Near the cristate saguaro is the biggest anthill I have ever seen in the United States: five feet in diameter and three feet tall crawling with a mass of red and black harvester ants. On such anthills as this the Yaqui and Apache, according to folklore, would crucify their enemies.

Down and across a broad sandy wash where the smoke tree, *Dalea spinosa,* flourishes. Well named, this hardy shrub seems to float on the air like a veil of wood smoke. Smoke trees grow only in washes primarily because more moisture is available here than on the harder, higher, stonier ground. But this is only a part of the explanation. Research has shown that, in order to break open and germinate, the seeds of the smoke tree must be rolled and tumbled along a rough sandy surface. The only force in nature that can provide such a service is the flash flood that rumbles down a dry stream bed during a summer storm. Stream action not only breaks open the seed coat, it also ensures that sufficient moisture will be present—at the right time of year—to sustain growth.

In the far southwest corner of the park, within 100 yards of the Mexican frontier, the road brings us to the oasis called Quitobaquito, the other important natural water source in Organ Pipe. It is also the only place in the park where large deciduous trees, in this case cottonwoods, grow. Always a refreshing sight, bright green in summer, gold in the fall, they stand out for miles against the pastel tones of the desert.

Quitobaquito is a pond fed by natural springs. It was the home of small Papago bands for many centuries. Later it became a popular way station on El Camino del Diablo, the road leading from northwest Mexico to southern California. Aside from a few unreliable springs and water pockets in the low mountains to the west, Quitobaquito was the last good water supply available to travelers until they reached the Colorado River some 100 miles farther west. Many are supposed to have died on that trail, some of thirst, some at the hands of Indians known as Areñero or Sand Papago. In the days of the forty-niners, when the California Gold Rush was at its height, many Europeans and Eastern Americans attempted this route. On the map it looked like a good short cut. Today a few of their graves can still be seen along the traces of the old road, little mounds of stone and wooden crosses way out in the Cabeza Prieta wilderness west of Organ Pipe.

I would make my patrol of the pond, answering tourist questions, picking up litter, fishing an occasional tin can out of the water. I would pause at the inlet to the pond to look at the pupfish, lively, gleaming inch-long cyprinodonts adapted to life in the brackish water of desert streams; a rare sort of fish, they can be found only in Death Valley, in the Sonoita River (really a creek) south of Organ Pipe, here at Quitobaquito and in a very few other desert places such as Devil's Hole in Nevada. Fish experts say that pupfish are remnants of inhabitants of great inland seas that vanished a million years ago. This could be true.

I completed my patrol of Quitobaquito by emptying the garbage cans and cleaning out the rest rooms, then with my load of garbage reeking in the back of the pickup I would head eastward toward headquarters, rounding off the loop. If the sun was still high and the day young I usually made the turnoff at Senita Basin to check up on the cactus and our best elephant tree.

Senita cactus, also known as old man or grandfather cactus because of the graybeard spines at the crown of each branch, is one of the smaller giant cacti, reaching a height of 15 feet. Uncommon in Arizona, abundant in Sonora, senitas are rough, rank, shaggy plants, grotesque, sunburned, a little ridiculous but good to look at and think about, nice to know. Like its big brothers the saguaro, organ pipe and cardon, the senita cactus can flourish only where the climate is hot and the freezing periods infrequent and brief. High in moisture content, it would burst like unsheathed plumbing if exposed to a prolonged freeze.

The elephant tree is something else. At maturity it too may reach 15 feet in height, but the one in Senita Basin is no taller than a shotgun. Rare in the U.S. (Mexico is its more familiar habitat), the elephant tree has a thick trunk, wide-branching limbs and a scaly, dead white, sometimes brassy, leprous bark. Another useless plant, no doubt, like the senita, without anything of economic value for man or beast. It looks like a monstrous turnip trying to struggle up out of the ground. What good is it? You can't eat it, use it or sell it. True—but there it is.

Besides interesting plant life Senita Basin contains the densest cluster of old mines and prospect holes in Organ Pipe; most of them I visited at least once a week.

My favorite was the one called Bluebird, long ago forgotten, now the home of Mexican hognose bats. Once I walked deep into the pitch blackness, hearing the rustle of thousands of membranous wings in the gloom before me. As I advanced the bats retreated farther and farther toward the end of the tunnel, a thickening concentration of alarm.

I was the one, however, who was blind as a bat. The mine tunnel takes several turns and gradually all daylight, even the finest trace of illumination, is left behind. We really have no conception of the meaning of darkness until we enter such a place. The interior of an unlit house, or a clouded-over starless night, is nothing like it. The blackness of a mine or cave has a palpable quality; you can feel it, as if it were a sort of fluid medium denser than air, lighter than water. You stop and listen, you stop and feel, you find yourself immersed in a disorienting nothingness. For a certain temperament fear and then panic must be no more than a heartbeat away.

Closer to the bats. I could hear them shrilling and fluttering, the thick sound of crowded wings. I switched on my flashlight and there they were, milling around in the dusty stagnant air, others hanging in clusters upside down from the tunnel roof. I advanced a few more steps, pressing them back, and then they rebelled and as a swarm exploded, rushing past, over, and around me toward the entrance of the mine. Always wear a hat and an old shirt on such expeditions—I emerged from the mine, blinking in the glare, pretty well covered on shoulders and head by a mantle of bat dung and guano dust.

After the mines, after Senita Basin, there was little to do but go home, although during the all-too-brief desert twilight, loveliest time of the day, I was often impelled to stay out until nightfall. All too brief? In the desert, generally speaking, when the sun goes down the light fades very quickly because there is little moisture in the air to refract and reflect light. Only for a few magical minutes does the half light linger over the hills and washes, rocks and trees, shrubs and sand, before it melts away on the current of the evening.

The Puerto Blanco Drive was one of several regular patrols. Another followed the Ajo mountain route which took me into the high rugged eastern portion of the monument. In addition there were half a dozen other more difficult patrols requiring four-wheel drive and foot travel. One of the best of the latter was the hike to the edge of the hatchet-blade peak of cliff-bound Kino, accessible by only one narrow, tricky, hard-to-find route. This is bighorn sheep country, lion country, hiking and scrambling country. And centipede country.

The biggest centipede I ever met in my life was the one I saw slipping into a water hole, or *tinaja,* near the foot of Kino Peak. It was a splendid shining golden-mahogany beast about 10 inches long, a bold handsome centipede, a warrior, with the concentrated sleek viciousness of an engine designed for destruction and nothing else. I fished it out of the water with a stick and tried to count the legs—not easy, for this warrior would not hold still. There seemed to be about 80: 40 on each side. All other features were present: long probing antennae, complicated mouth parts of double mandibles and double maxillae, the front legs with their poisonous fangs, the feet like claws.

I know it's unjust and irrational, but I have never been able to overcome a definite sense of horror when confronting these armor-plated arthropods—scorpions, tarantulas, centipedes. This one below Kino Peak made me believe in the Devil. I turned it loose and watched it scurry off over the rock, a miniaturized tyrannic tank, bound for whatever happened in its way.

The best place to see bighorn sheep in the wild was up in the Ajo Range. Almost every time I went hiking there I'd see at least one or two. Always by chance. Once on Diaz Peak my friend John De Puy and I came upon a herd of nine. They were browsing on the brush, upwind from us, when we came around a ledge of rock and saw them. We stopped instantly and the sheep, unaware of our presence, continued to feed. We stood for what seemed like a long time but was probably only minutes, contemplating those lean, muscular, magnificent animals; one was an old patriarch of a ram, with massive horns curling back, around and forward in a full spiral; he must have been five feet long, three high at the shoulder, and weighed more than 200 pounds. May he live to reproduce his kind many times over and not end up, stuffed and glass-eyed, on the pine-paneled wall of some head collector's home.

Tiring a bit, one of us made a movement. At once the horned heads went up, the sheep saw us and sprang away in unison over the rocks with easy grace, vanishing down the mountainside. We were on the summit; they had nowhere to go but downhill.

A long-familiar landmark of Organ Pipe Cactus National Monument, the Bull Pasture (top center) juts out of the side of Mount Ajo like an immense hanging shelf. In years gone by this plateau's flat grassy terrain provided good grazing for cattle herds—after they had arduously climbed more than a mile above the desert floor to get there.

One day we climbed Montezuma's Head, a great eroded butte in the northeast corner of Organ Pipe. A first time for me, an oft-repeated tradition for the other rangers—Bill Hoy, Jim Carrico, Hal Coss. We started early in the morning, Jim and Bill leading the way. It is a technical climb, for which ropes and pitons are desirable, and my stomach was full of butterflies. Not too bad up to the shoulder of the monster, although there are certain hairy pitches on the route that make me sick to think about even now: I mean the sort of place on the rock where, if you glance down between your legs, you're likely to see a redtail hawk sailing past a hundred feet below.

We worked our way around the shoulder of the Head and came to a place called the Mantle. One look and I resolved to go no farther—but kept the resolution to myself for the moment. We had a choice of ascents: the first up a chimney, the second around and up the edge of the Mantle. The chimney looked much cozier to me, but the others agreed it took too long.

We roped up. A little numbly, for I'm no climber, I allowed myself to be attached to the rest of the party. Jim took the lead, stepping lightly along a slick ledge about six inches wide, about a thousand feet above the abyss. All that empty, vacant, fantastic space below, yearning toward our fragile human bodies with hypnotic magnetism. Jim reached a point where the little ledge petered out. From there the route led straight upward, by way of a single tiny handhold just a short distance beyond the reach of a man of average height. In order to gain that grip of solid rock it would be necessary for Jim to make a little leap up the face of the bulge before him.

We had him well belayed from the side and below. If he jumped and missed, we'd be able to stop his fall within 30 or 40 feet. He'd probably break no more than a few ribs, a leg, maybe a neck—nothing serious.

He jumped. And caught the handhold, as we all knew all along he would. He went on up, found a good belaying point and secured the climb for the rest of us. From there on it was a routine scramble. We reached the bald summit of Montezuma's Head, a dome of rock sloping away on all sides toward eagles' nests and the kinds of cliffs nightmares are made of.

"What's to do up here?" said Hal Coss, looking bored.

Things do not always turn out so well in this Organ Pipe desert, however. On February 3, 1971, we lost a visitor. On that day a young woman named Carol Turner, age 32, went for a solo walk up into an area of the

Ajo Range called the Bull Pasture, and disappeared, vanished as if from the face of the earth. She was an experienced hiker, in good bodily and mental health, a physical education instructor at the University of New Mexico—and her fate remains a complete mystery. So far not a trace of her has been found.

The case began with a ranger finding a note under the windshield wiper of Carol Turner's car, the note stating that she had gone for a hike up to the Bull Pasture and planned to return the same day. When she did not return on schedule a search was begun at once, expanded rapidly and continued for 12 days.

A second note was found in the trail register box at the top end of the Bull Pasture trail, addressed to anyone, unsigned but clearly in Carol Turner's handwriting:

"Hi, if you have binocs—look for a white shirt or yellow windbreaker across the way and say Hello."

The first day's search was carried out by the Organ Pipe ranger staff, but when the missing woman could not be found, reinforcements were called in, including Papago trackers, a United States Air Force helicopter, the Ajo town police, the border patrol, the county sheriff's department and the entire volunteer search and rescue team of Pima County. At the height of the search a total of 130 men were involved. But nothing was found. On February 15 Hal Coss and Bill Hoy, searching an area beyond a volcanic outcropping called the Sphinx, thought they detected the odor of decomposing flesh but could not find the source of the smell. On February 16 the search was called off officially, on the grounds that the woman could not possibly be still alive after 12 days without food or water in the desert mountains. The rangers and maintenance men of Organ Pipe have carried on periodic searches ever since then, in hopes of finding at least some bodily remains and solving the mystery, but without success.

In his official report on the matter Rod Broyles, then chief ranger at Organ Pipe, wrote that "there is no evidence of suicide, foul play or a planned disappearance." The conclusion is that Carol Turner probably fell or slipped, injured herself and crawled into one of the many small caves or brushy crevices in the cliffs for shelter from the cold and wind. Since the searchers the next day heard no hint of a human cry for aid it also seems likely that she lost consciousness soon after her accident and died of shock, bleeding and exposure.

The walk up to the Bull Pasture is one of the loveliest and most rewarding in the entire monument. The trail climbs steeply from the Ajo Drive parking lot, winding through a narrow canyon, among boulders, past a great variety of desert plants, up over a ridge and along the base of great yellowish cliffs to a high point overlooking the place for which the trail is named.

The name is strictly historical, based on the fact that an early rancher kept cattle here, and conveys little of the character of the place. It is a grassy basin, walled in on the east by the ramparts of Mount Ajo and surrounded on all other sides except the trail route by precipitous drop-offs hundreds of feet high. It is a natural corral, requiring only some 20 feet of fence at one place to keep livestock penned in.

Worn across the bottom of the Bull Pasture are small ravines, with deep *tinajas* eroded in the red rock. Water can usually be found in the bottom of the deepest *tinajas,* even during the dry months of May and June, and sometimes, after summer storms or winter rains, the ravines come alive with running streams and brief, splashing waterfalls.

Since it has been free of cattle for many years the Bull Pasture is one of the few places in Organ Pipe Cactus National Monument where the visitor can see a bit of nature in its pure state. Here the grass grows knee high, the agave, the yucca and the ocotillo flourish, and the flowers, during the spring and autumn months, if the rains and temperatures have been propitious, brighten the fields with acres of color. The light seems a little more dramatic here than anywhere else in Organ Pipe —the sunrises, the sunsets, the moonrises, the stars a little more brilliant—and the air is almost always clean and good. There is something sweet, calming and benign in the general stillness, a quiet never disturbed by any sounds more harsh than those of the wind rushing through the tall grass, the music of falling water, the scream of a hawk. We have few places like this remaining in our poor, pillaged, squandered, ravished Arizona; there are not many that a man or woman could find better for a last long walk under the sun and sky, through the wind, into the earth.

The Lavish, Frugal Cacti

Though cacti are native to many corners of the Western Hemisphere, from Patagonia to Canada, they have reached a peak of development and diversification in the Sonoran Desert. Botanists have listed more than 140 species of cactus in this region, from the stately organ pipe (right) to the squat, spiny teddy bear cholla —and more are still being found.

Some of the most typical cacti of the Sonoran Desert are shown on the following pages in pictures taken at Arizona's Organ Pipe Cactus National Monument. In the sheer variety of their forms and functions, these species sum up the present life style of the whole cactus family.

The origins of this bizarre family are shrouded in mystery. Botanists believe that the commonest forms of cacti extant today probably evolved from primitive jungle plants native to several areas of Central and South America. The ancestral plants had numerous large leaves and woody stems, but their descendants, in adjusting to life in the desert have literally reshaped themselves to fit their environment, increasing their bulk and reducing the surface area they expose to sun and desiccating winds. In making this adaptation, cacti stopped bearing leaves; they could no longer afford these broad-surfaced appendages because of their spendthrift way with water; a leafy plant that has 100 times the surface area of a barrel cactus of equal weight loses moisture roughly 6,000 times as quickly.

When the cacti dispensed with foliage, their stems and branches, green with chlorophyll, took over the leaves' work of manufacturing food. This arrangement permits the cacti, drawing energy from almost constant sunlight and moisture from their water-storing interior pulp, to function all year round and to flower even during lengthy droughts.

Many other adaptations play a vital role in the frugal existence of the cacti. Their shallow, widespread root systems absorb maximum moisture in a region of brief rainstorms and thin, quick-draining soil. The waxy finish on their tough skins retards moisture loss, and their armament of sharp spines affords some protection from sun, wind and from the depredations of hungry, thirsty desert creatures.

Thanks to these ingenious mechanisms, the cacti, overcoming rigors that offer only a slender margin for life, are considered one of the greatest successes in the plant world.

A fusion of strength and grace, this large organ pipe cactus reaches a height of 20 feet with its tallest stems. Each expandable water-storing stem is supported by a woody framework and covered by a pleated skin with 12 to 19 vertical ridges resembling welts. The ridges are studded with dark areoles. Complex structures possessed only by cacti, the areoles produce clusters of spines and, high up on the organ pipe's stems, a scattering of fragrant night-blooming flowers.

A LOFTY ORGAN PIPE CACTUS

SPINES GROWING FROM AREOLES

FLOWERS THAT BLOOM BY NIGHT

A YOUNG PRICKLY-PEAR CACTUS

A RIPE FRUIT

NEWLY OPENED BLOSSOMS

PRICKLY-PEAR ARMOR

A BEE IN A DARKENING FLOWER

The Tough, Homely Prickly Pear

Prickly pears are the hardiest, most adaptable plants in the cactus family. Plain and unimpressive—though they have vivid red fruit and magnificent flowers that darken subtly from one day to the next—they grow in a sprawling succession of water-storing pads, protected by clusters of long spines and short barbed bristles called glochids. Capable of thriving in the poorest soil, these plants grow faster than their larger, handsomer relatives, reaching full size and strength in five to 10 years.

The prickly pears' vigor is based on a highly efficient root system. A tapering taproot anchors the plant, and a wide network of shallow roots rapidly soaks up rain water during the brief desert storms. In winter some species develop swollen roots; these take over the moisture-storing function of the pads, which are thus spared damage from freezing. The prickly pears' roots also help stabilize the thin, loose desert soil; the widespread roots of one species, the starvation prickly pear, are credited with keeping huge quantities of soil from being blown away by the winds that scour the arid Southwest.

Thanks to their toughness and adaptability, the prickly pears have achieved wider distribution than any other group of plants in the cactus family. They grow in sun-scorched flats and in chilly mile-high uplands, and can be found in all of the contiguous United States except Maine, New Hampshire and Vermont.

The Bulky, Pulpy Barrel Cactus

Tagged with as many nicknames as an aggregation of athletes, the family of barrel cacti—as their best-known common name suggests—are thick and squat. Even the tallest, which may reach 10 feet, look shorter than they are because of their water-bloated girth. The nicknames come from the many idiosyncrasies found among various species: some are called compass barrels because they naturally lean toward the sunny southwest or fishhook barrels for their long curved spines.

But few nicknames reflect the whole truth. Barrel cacti are not, as desert folklore would have it, filled to the brim with crystal-clear water, ever available to save the lives of dehydrated travelers. When the top of a barrel cactus is lopped off, the plant is found to be filled with a soft mass of tiny storage cells that hold moisture like the tissue of a sponge.

The shape of the barrel cactus —and of many other cacti—depends entirely on this soft cellular interior, whose changing moisture content causes the expansion and contraction of the plant's pleated skin. The pulp, scooped out and squeezed, yields a thick, sticky liquid that is slow to evaporate and so bitter that a traveler would have to be desperate to swallow a mouthful. But when the pulp is cut into cubes and boiled in sugar syrup, it makes a sweet that is something like watermelon preserves—hence another of the plant's nicknames: candy cactus.

A BARREL CACTUS BLOOM

A COVILLE BARREL CACTUS

MATURE FLESHY FRUIT

A CLOSE-UP OF SPINES

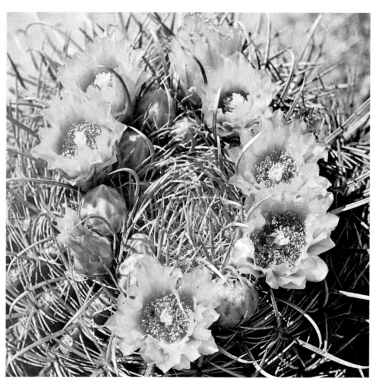

A CLUSTER OF NEW BLOSSOMS

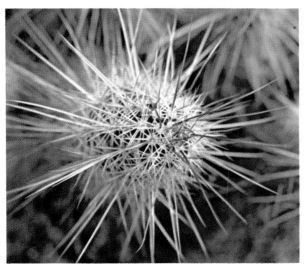

A HEDGEHOG CACTUS' QUILL-LIKE SPINES

A MANY-STEMMED HEDGEHOG

A SMALL-BLOSSOMED FENDLER'S HEDGEHOG

FLOWERS OF A GOLDEN HEDGEHOG

The Hedgehog's Prickly Beauty

The hedgehog cactus, named for the resemblance of its long spines to a porcupine's quills, produces some of the most beautiful flowers in the entire cactus family. The blossoms of most hedgehog cacti are elegant, brilliant and spectacularly large in relation to the size of the plant. Few hedgehogs grow more than 10 inches tall, yet many species put forth flowers that measure three inches in diameter when fully opened. One species, the comb hedgehog, has blossoms five or six inches across —growing on a plant no more than nine inches tall. The hedgehogs' flowers may be white, yellow or pale green, but in most species the blooms combine red and blue in varying hues, producing almost every purplish tone from a pale lavender to a dark magenta verging on black. The petals have a delicate, satiny sheen that heightens the blaze of color, even in small-flowered species such as the Fendler's hedgehog (opposite, bottom). Some species have hundreds of stems to a single plant, and each stem may have several flowers blooming at once.

As a further decorative touch, the flower color of many species is subtly shaded from dark at the base to light at the petals' tips. One species, the golden hedgehog (left), sets off its pale lavender-pink flower with reproductive organs of contrasting color: dark green female stigmas at the center of the flower and male stamens of a delicate whitish yellow.

A RANK OF SPINES

A SENITA CLUMP

A BALD STEM TOP

A NIGHT-BLOOMING SENITA FLOWER

The Slender Gray-whiskered Senita

Seen from a distance, the rare senita cactus is easily mistaken for a towering organ pipe cactus. But the senita's columnar stems, armed with linear ranks of spines, are usually shorter (about 10 feet high), thinner and more numerous than those of the organ pipe. The senita's tapering tops are occasionally bald and sunburned, but usually they are tufted with gray whiskery spines. Like the organ pipe, the senita is a night-blooming species; but its flowers are smaller and more plentiful than the blooms of the organ pipe.

The senita's long, slender stems help to explain the species' local rarity. Except for their tough skin and woody framework, the thin stems consist entirely of spongy water-storing tissue that makes the plant highly vulnerable to damage from freezing, which can prune back the stems or even prove fatal to the plant. Partly because of this frailty, the senita's normal habitat is the frost-free desert region south of the Mexican border.

But in Arizona's Organ Pipe Cactus National Monument there are some senitas that manage to withstand occasional cold snaps. Their ability to survive freezing, a dramatic proof of the adaptability of cacti, is explained by the fact that senitas in Arizona have thicker stems than those in Mexico; these senitas have increased their mass in relation to their surface area in order to conserve enough warmth for survival.

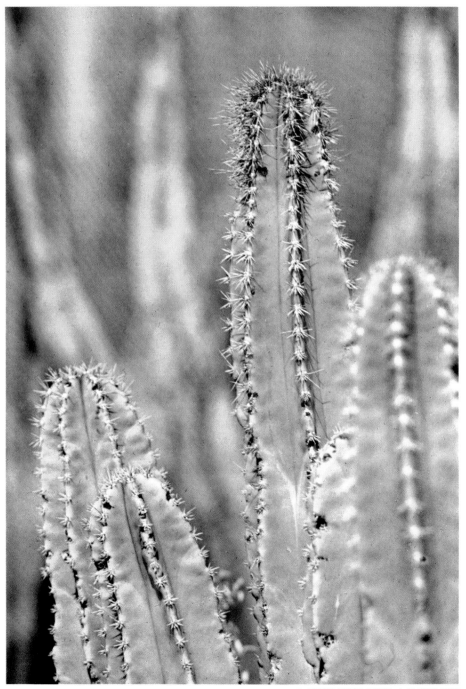

A SPINY STEM WITH A HAIRY TOP

The Bristling, Brittle Teddy Bear

The chollas are the prickliest plants in the cactus family, and the prickliest of their kind is the small and shrubby teddy bear cholla. Paradoxically, the teddy bear's fierce armament accounts for its disarming nickname: its straw-colored spines and glochids are so numerous and close-set that the entire plant looks furry, especially when it glistens in a halo of bright sunlight.

To make the teddy bear even more formidable, it shares with the other chollas a brittleness that has proved painful to many a careless traveler. Its water-storing branches grow in short, thick segments called joints, which break off so easily on contact that they seem almost to leap up to impale a victim. Hence various species are popularly called "jumping" chollas, though of course they have no means of self-propulsion.

For all its spiky hostility to most creatures, the teddy bear provides protection for a few of them. The ingenious cactus wren constructs its nest securely in the heart of the plant; the pack rat fortifies its nest with piled-up cholla joints.

While functioning as a defensive weapon, the chollas' barbs also aid in the propagation of the species. By breaking off and hooking a ride on passing animals, the bristling joints are widely dispersed. Wherever a joint falls to the ground, it needs only adequate moisture and warm soil temperatures to put down roots and grow into a complete new plant.

A FLOWER GUARDED BY SPIKY ARMAMENT

DY BEAR CHOLLA

A FORMIDABLE DEFENSE

A FURRY CLUMP OF TEDDY BEAR JOINTS

TEDDY BEAR CHOLLAS UNDER A NOONDAY SUN

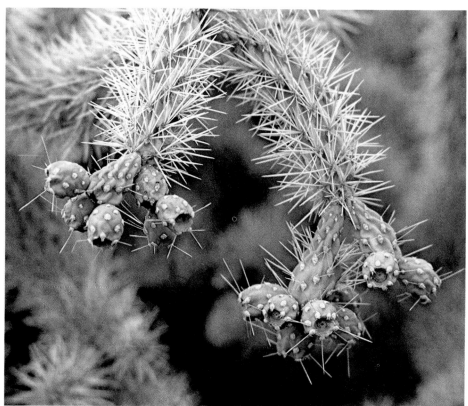

CHAINS OF CHOLLA FRUIT

The Varied Tribe of Chollas

While all chollas share such basic characteristics as spiny joints, the various species differ radically in growth patterns and appearance. In contrast to the bristle-covered teddy bear cholla, the buckhorn cholla (so called because its water-storing branches resemble a deer's antlers) is only lightly armed with spines and glochids. Some full-grown cholla species are less than a foot tall, while the chain fruit chollas resemble trees, often measuring 12 feet in height and seven inches in diameter at the base of the woody trunk.

The chain fruit cholla is further distinguished by a striking peculiarity that inspired its name: the species bears its fruit in long festoons that sometimes touch the ground. The process that forms each chain begins with a flower that may vary in color from pink to purple, depending on the composition of the soil. After the flower withers away, an egg-shaped green fruit develops and usually remains on the plant; the next year—and the next—the fruit, still green and still growing, produces a flower and it, in turn, produces another fruit. Chains of fruit with 12 or 14 links are not uncommon.

Curiously, the fruit of this species contains only a few seeds, which are generally infertile, or no seeds at all. Yet the chain fruit cholla is in no danger of dying out; even a seedless fruit will take root just as readily as a broken-off joint when it falls on warm soil and is moistened by rain.

A CHAIN FRUIT CHOLLA

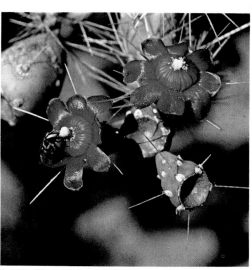

A BEE ON A CHOLLA FLOWER

BUCKHORN CHOLLA IN BLOOM

A BUCKHORN BRANCH

SPRAWLING BUCKHORN CHOLLA

4/ The Sacred Peak

*Nearly every striking feature of this special world
…goes back ultimately to the grand fact of dryness — the
dryness of the ground, of the air, of the whole sum-total.*

JOSEPH WOOD KRUTCH/ *THE VOICE OF THE DESERT*

Papaguería, the Papago Indian Reservation in the heart of Arizona's So-noran Desert, is a place of hungry cows and haggard horses, fat buzzards and horned toads, flash floods and cactus forests. It is a place of mud villages with names unpronounceable to the alien tongue: Schuchk, Vaya Chin, Supi Oidak, Chukut Kuk, Kom Vo, Gu Komelik, Sil Nakya, Pan Tak and Hickiwan. And it is a land of mountains. Papaguería is the place of the Comobabi Mountains, the Quijotoa Mountains and, highest and most important, the number one holy one, home of the god I'itoi, big green island in the desert sea, sticking up against the sky like a great tooth—Baboquivari.

All my life I had wanted to ascend that sacred mountain, most won-derful of remote lost places on the maps of boyhood. (Those maps. I used to read them as others read fairy tales, comic books and the funny papers; for me maps were equally magical. Who or what for example lived in Gunlock, Utah? Wolf Hole, Arizona? Bedrock, Colorado? Pie Town, New Mexico? And what was life like there, how did it feel, how did the morning light slant across the hills, what went on in the dead heat of a summer afternoon, where were the people when the fool moon rose at sunset like a great big platinum cymbal and simply hung there for a while, mute, potent, an unstruck gong above the hills? Who would record it all if I never got there in time? A serious question.)

So, a few years ago a friend, Dave Rehfield, and I staggered at midnight from a party, stumbled into a car, drove 80 miles south-southwest to the eastern base of Baboquivari, slept on the cold ground till dawn, woke up sick and beat, ate some tuna straight from a tin and started up the mountain.

We passed first a small ranch where yellow-eyed hound dogs barked passionately at our heels, earning their daily feed. We ignored them, plunged into oak thickets and juniper jungles, found a path and followed it upward to the crest of a ridge that seemed to lead to the base of the final peak. By the time we got that far it was late afternoon and the big granite tooth of Baboquivari seemed as far away as ever. Nevertheless we trudged on, up the ridge, into more thickets of scrub oak, tangles of thorny acacia, open places mined with prickly pear and Schott's agave. The October heat was sickening—a fierce, sullen resistance—and the trail petered out into an unfollowable maze of cattle paths and deer runs, through thorny tunnels under the brush. The sun was going down, a chill crept into the air and then into our bones. Hungover, exhausted, hungry, we gave up and retreated back down the long ridge to the ranch, the dogs, the road, our car.

Baboquivari had defeated our first expedition. But I knew that we would try again. I knew that Justice William O. Douglas had once climbed this mountain and if he could I could.

It was two years later, in the month of December, that another friend, John De Puy, and I drove to the western side of the mountain, in Papaguería, and camped at the foot of the trail, fortifying ourselves with steak and beer, coffee and cognac. Through the afternoon the skies had been cloudy, prophesying storm, but after sundown the clouds went away and all the desert stars came out.

There was a little formal campground here beneath Baboquivari's western flank, at the end of the road, with concrete picnic tables, fireplaces with grills, an abandoned ruin of what appeared to have been a caretaker's residence, and an official greeting sign from the Papago tribe in big bold hand-lettered red characters:

> Keep America Beautiful
> Pick Up Your Trash Before Leaving
> THIS means YOU!!
> Thank you!

Inevitably, scattered all about were the tin cans and foil wrappers, plastic plates, paper diapers, worn-out socks and old tennis shoes of those who come to where such signs are found. Through the garbage and under the spreading mesquite trees ran a trickle of a brook fed by melting snows above, a meager stream but musical, splashing over the rocks and sand and clods of old cow dung.

Cattle and cattle tracks were everywhere. The campground was badly overgrazed, as is the entire Papago Reservation. As is most of the West, come to think of it. When the grass is gone and the land becomes too tough for cattle we'll see herds of goats browsing on the cactus, as they do in North Africa, Mesopotamia, Crete—followed finally by teams of archeologists.

The starving had already begun. On hand to welcome us when we entered this derelict campground was a little yellow dog, a shaggy undersized mutt so obviously abandoned and unwanted, so wretched, so painfully servile, so conspicuously worthless, that even our cold hearts were faintly touched. We gave him the wax from our Edam cheese. He gulped it down without even tasting it. We gave him the butcher paper that had wrapped the steaks, nice and bloody and greasy, and he devoured it.

We stared at this voracious cur, impressed despite ourselves by his enthusiasm for survival. He stared back at us, the black shoe-button eyes shining with faith and hope, the stub of a tail wagging furiously. This was on December 20 and the spirit of Christmas stirred feebly in our bosoms. We retrieved one of the plastic plates nearby and poured the dog some beer. He lapped it up at once. We threw him a chunk of gristle and fat from one of the steaks and it vanished in mid-air, inside a sudden blur of yellowish hair.

I suggested then that the most merciful thing we could do would be to beat the little chap over the head with a rock until he was dead. My friend De Puy crossed himself, looking apprehensively at the mountain hanging above us, and muttered something about I'itoi the god of Baboquivari. He sliced off a portion of his steak and tossed it dogward. Again the miraculous disappearance. I was shamed into doing the same and so we had an unwanted dog on our hands and souls for the rest of the night and all the next day. We crawled into our mummy bags and dreamed of cheerful things.

Sometime before dawn we were awakened by the crowing of roosters from a nearby Papago rancheria. We rose and fumbled about in the dark, warmed up a sort of breakfast, packed our packs and shambled off up the trail. We figured on a long day; I carried a 120-foot rope, for use on rock, across my shoulders.

It would be a 3,000-foot climb from the big cactus belt where we started to the piñon-juniper zone at the base of Baboquivari's bare peak. On the way upward I could mark the degree of our ascent not only by the trembling of my knees but also by the successive changes in the character of the vegetation.

First, the mesquite forest, a dense jungle of thorny, scrubby little trees, their numbers a sure result of overgrazing. Good for firewood and fence posts, the mesquite tree also produces a kind of bean that makes a nutritious food for both animals and man; for many centuries it was one of the staples of the Papago diet. On the other hand, where the mesquite grows thick the grass cannot; when the cattle strip off the ground cover the mesquite forest moves in and takes over; the cattle depart. Thus what is gained in beans is lost in beef, and which is better only time will show.

Towering above the mesquite is the great saguaro cactus. Burned by the sun and battered by storms, scarred by disease, bacteria, mammals and birds, some of these old giants have been here since the time of the American Revolution. They show it. Yet still alive, still flowering each May, they keep on reproducing. Or trying to. They produce their quota of seeds. The trouble is that swarms of hungry cattle, infesting so much of the Southwest, tend to trample out the young saguaro before they can take hold. Only those seedlings lucky enough to germinate and take root within the shelter of a nurse tree—a mesquite, ironwood or paloverde—where they are protected from foraging cattle and rodents and too much direct sunlight, are able to reach maturity.

The saguaro grows very slowly, sometimes taking nine to ten years to reach a height of six inches, about 30 years to reach five feet, 150 years to reach 35 feet. A saguaro may live, it has been estimated, for 200 years, grow to a height of 50 feet and weigh as much as seven tons. The weight of a particular saguaro varies from time to time, depending upon the amount of moisture available to the plant. Because of its fluted, columnar structure, the saguaro is able to expand when water is available for storage and to contract when the drought returns. The water-storing tissue of the plant makes up 75 to 95 per cent of its gross weight. Because of its great moisture-retaining capacity the saguaro can survive the most prolonged and severe dry spells, continue growth and carry on reproduction.

Like many plants the saguaro reproduces through flowering and pollination, a process that seems to require the agency of bats, moths and birds. The flowers usually appear in late May, large creamy-white blossoms clustered on the tip of the central trunk and on the tip of each branch. If fertilization occurs, the flowers produce an oval-shaped, bright red fruit about two to three inches long, without spines, resembling a watermelon in flavor, and containing over 1,000 tiny black seeds. This fruit is a popular item in the diet not only of birds and other flying creatures but also of man; the Papago Indians have traditionally harvested saguaro fruit by using long poles to knock the fruit to the ground. It can then be eaten raw or dried for storage, or ground up, allowed to ferment and made into a kind of cactus wine.

The saguaro's prospects for survival, as a species, seem only fair. Cattle grazing continues to take its toll. Near towns and cities, land-clearing projects, agriculture and housing developments have eliminated entire stands. Some botanists believe the plant is also being attacked by new forms of disease. Saving the saguaro will require more study and research and better protection, especially in the national monuments, where a new breed of cactus poachers dig up large numbers of healthy plants that are in demand as decorations for suburban lawns.

Up the trail we walked through thickets of ocotillo, that weird, Martian, spidery thing, and higher on the mountainside we entered the zone of the agaves. Here are the century plants, in various stages of development from baby rosettes close to the ground to the 15-foot expired stalks of last season's dead.

The century plant does not live a century; it only seems that way if you are sitting around waiting for it to bloom. Fifteen to 20 years is a normal lifespan, concluded by a flowering—the only one—and death. Year after year the plant has grown slowly, developing its base of heavy rigid leaves, each tipped with a sharp red spine. In the center of the plant the leaves remain folded together like the heart of an artichoke, concealing the agave's core. Finally one spring the supreme moment arrives: the inner leaves part and within a few days a great tumescent stalk rises to a height of up to 15 feet. Then it blooms—a loosely clustered pyramid of large, showy golden flowers at the tip of the stalk. This glorious blooming time is short. In only a few weeks the flowers fade, the stalk dries up and by the end of the summer the entire plant is dead. But it has accomplished the purpose for which the sacrifice was made: the flowers are succeeded by pods containing the hardy, dried seeds of the next generation.

Here at Baboquivari, the clock-face, or dollar-joint, prickly pear cactus, so named for the symmetric round shape of the succulent joints or

A mile below 7,730-foot-high Baboquivari, mesquite, acacias and a looming saguaro share a rugged slope that rises from the desert floor.

pads, is perhaps the most prevalent of the cacti. The purplish fruit, which tastes a bit like pomegranate, is very sweet and seedy. The clusters of fine hairs on the skin of each "pear" can be removed by rubbing it through sand.

The trail paralleled a ravine for about half a mile and here we saw more typical desert plants like the hackberry, an evergreen shrub (sometimes growing to tree height) that provides occasional fruit for birds and small mammals. Also present was the acacia, both the white-thorn and the catclaw. The second is well named: the small curved claws, exactly like those of a cat, will sink themselves equally well into cloth or flesh and cling there, halting the unwary traveler's progress. Like mesquite, ironwood and paloverde, the acacias are members of the great pea family, the third largest group of flowering plants in the world (after the sunflower family and the orchid family).

We passed through stands of jojobas, shrubs that provide good browsing for deer and cattle. Among the jojobas grow other shrubs: white ratany, or crimson beak, the roots of which were boiled by Indians and pioneers to make a medicinal tea; coursetia, or baby bonnet, named for the shape of the small white flowers; and the fairy duster,

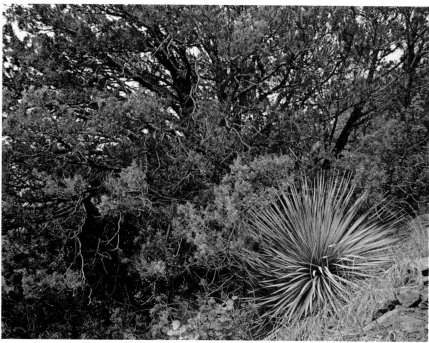

A JUNIPER TREE AND A SOTOL PLANT

LIVE OAKS, JUNIPERS AND PINONS

also known as false mesquite or calliandra, good browse for game and livestock. All of these shrubs are likewise members of the pea family.

Here also was the shrub called Mormon tea or Mexican tea or green ephedra, an odd plant because the stems appear completely leafless and because the seeds are contained in primitive cones that relate it to such ancient—and more common—forms of plant life as pines and other conifers. Unlike the pine, the Mormon tea shrub carries chlorophyll not in its scalelike leaves but in its green stems, a supply sufficient to maintain the food-producing process of photosynthesis. Mormon tea is thought to have therapeutic powers. I have brewed it myself, out of curiosity, boiling the stems and sipping the resultant tea. I found the flavor very bitter, which explains its curative reputation: anything that tastes so bad must be good for you.

The trail switchbacked still higher. Now and then we caught a glimpse of the great rock peak of Baboquivari soaring far above and far away, too far, seemingly inaccessible, a likely home for a desert god. We plodded onward, slowly and steadily, pausing at times to rest for a minute but not sitting down, which is much too tiring on a long uphill hike. Hard to explain but true. Only the slow and steady plod, based on

At different stages of the ascent to the top of Baboquivari, marked changes appear in the type and density of vegetation. A variety of tough plants and trees flourishes at about 4,600 feet (far left). The trees thin out around 6,000 feet (center) and diminish in size to shrubby dwarfs (below) at 7,000 feet, just below the bald, rocky summit.

SCRUB OAKS AND HARDY MOUNTAIN SHRUBS

heart and will as much as legs and lungs, can get you all the way.

Higher and higher. The vegetation continued to change. We saw a dark and scraggly thing called limber bush or, by the Mexicans, *sangre de drago*—dragon's blood—because of the reddish sap, sometimes used as a dye by the Indians. Here was the hopbush or switch sorrel, a member of the soapberry family, containing certain toxic substances that the Indians used as a poison to catch fish. A bright green shrub found in this zone is the red-berry buckthorn, with oily leaves and bright red fruit, sometimes utilized by the Papago in making a form of desert pemmican; they would mix the berries with meat into a highly nutritious, compact food easily carried on long marches.

From time to time we saw signs of coyotes, javelinas, jack rabbits, deer along the trail; red-tailed hawks and prairie falcons wheeled in the sky; flocks of piñon jays, juncoes and chickadees in the woods. We reached a saddle on the ridge below the peak and entered what seemed to me the most beautiful plant community on the mountain. Here, under the red and orange cliffs of ancient volcanic rocks, were green groves of Ajo oaks, piñon pines and junipers, with drifts of December snow stretching across the trail.

The Ajo oak was not classified until 1954. It seldom grows more than 30 feet tall but is nevertheless a true oak tree, producing acorns, nutritious and fattening for wildlife, and a good long-burning very hot fuel much in demand for heating and cooking among the Indians. Mixed with the oaks were two kinds of juniper: the one-seed, or monosperm, juniper and the alligator juniper, so called because of the hidelike texture of the bark. Beyond the junipers and oaks we walked gratefully into the shade of a pure stand of piñon pine, where the air smelled damp and resinous, and banks of ferns grew between the snowdrifts. It was a cool, dark place, high above the desert, refreshing after the wearying dust and glare below.

The trail now followed the shaded northern side of the ridge where the snow became a problem. The crust on the surface was not quite hard enough to support a man's weight; with every step we broke through the crust and sank in to the knees. Step-plunge, step-plunge —an awkward gait. But we carried on. The peak seemed much nearer and the day was still not old. We crossed over the ridge again into most welcome sunshine, a grassy slope with a vast view to the south, east and west. We stopped to eat our lunch.

Now we had to acknowledge that the yellow cur had followed us all the way; here he came, sniffing, whining, tail vibrating, eyes shining with a piteous hope. We had no choice but to share our lunch with him, suspecting that this dog might be much more than he appeared, might well be some disguised form of the spirit of the mountain—an avatar —sent down by I'itoi to test our souls. We gave the wretch the leftovers of our leftover steak.

Onward. The trail wound under thickets of oak and piñon pine, the snowdrifts became continuous and deeper. At places we sank in to our hips. On hands and knees we crawled over the largest of the drifts and came finally, at last, thank God, to the base of the great peak. Above was good, solid rock.

From here the route led along the base of a cliff, and then upward at 45 degrees toward the summit. After the brush and snow it was a great pleasure to plant our boots on real rock again and walk normally. We scraped the ice from the boot lugs and began to scramble. There was some ice on the rock, but it lay in patches and we found it easy to avoid, at least in the beginning.

At the first steep pitch we came to the ruins of a wooden stairway built in the 1930s by the CCC—the New Deal's Civilian Conservation Corps. The stairway now was nothing but fragments of splintered wood, studded with rusty spikes, more dangerous than the bare rock to which it was still partially anchored. We passed to the side of it, continued climbing over the rocks, traversed to the north side of the peak and encountered the combination of brush and snow again. More struggle, working through a tunnel of a path in the scrub oak thickets, until we came to the second rocky pitch. The little yellow dog was still with us, following close on our heels.

At this point the mountain assumed a more serious aspect. It began to look like rope country—not to say ice-ax country, and we had no ice ax. Not even a screw driver. We shuffled to the top of the last snowdrift and stood looking up at about 100 feet of rugged rock cliff, much of it glistening with ice, rising upward at an angle close to the vertical, with a little bench or shelf every now and then. Near the top we could see the remains of another wooden stairway built by the CCC—far beyond our reach this time. In between was an intricate puzzle of toe holds and fingertip grips that we had to solve in order to climb any higher. Since we were both strictly amateur rock climbers the prospect seemed dim. Was dim.

What were the stairways for? There was time for that question while we picked at the ice with our fingernails. The answer is that someone

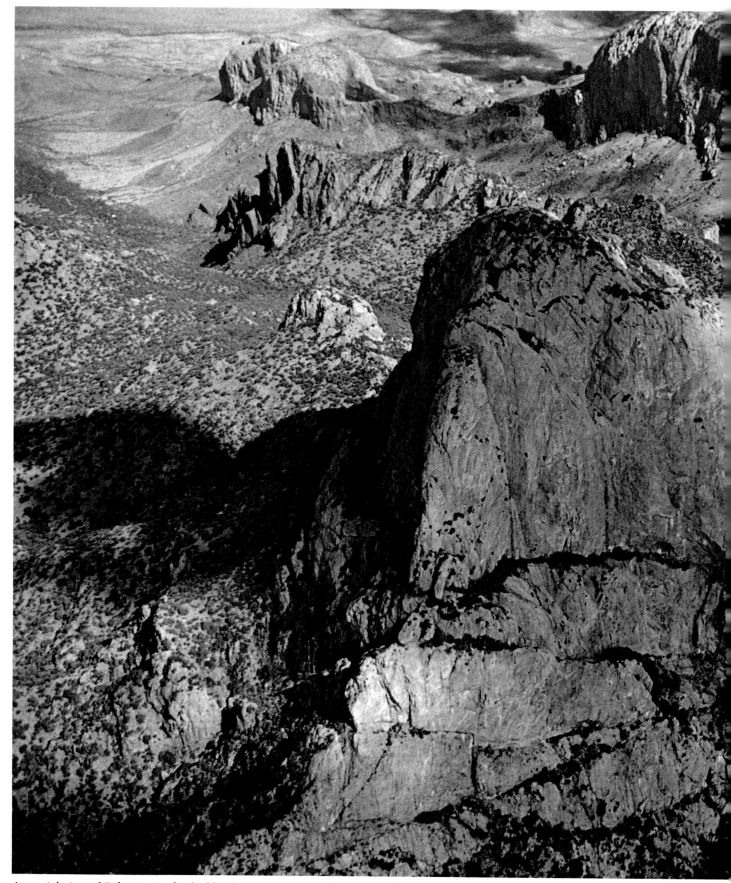

An aerial view of Baboquivari, backed by the narrow, 40-mile-long range of which it is part, reveals sharp faults and almost perpendicular mountain's southeast face. Revered in Papago Indian legend as the home of a desert god, the peak also poses a strong challenge to climbers.

in the CCC decided that there should be a fire lookout station on top of Baboquivari. Lord knows it was high enough—7,730 feet above sea level, approximately 5,000 feet above the surrounding cactus desert. At great effort and expense the trail was built up the mountainside, the lumber for the stairways laboriously trucked in, carpentered together and hung on the cliffs, a frame shack erected on the summit of the mountain, and even a telephone line strung on poles the whole way from base to peak. The work was done.

Then someone realized that there was no forest to look at, or even to speak of, from the heights of Baboquivari. Nothing around and below, for hundreds of square miles, but the poor, overgrazed, trampled Papago desert. No trees but scrubby mesquite and paloverde, no grass but poverty weed and snakeweed, nothing worth setting fire to—or building a fire station to protect. One imagines the hush that must have fallen over the conversation as the government officials gazed out from the peak upon that lovely, forlorn, splendid and desolate wasteland. Since then, over the decades, the weather and the hikers have gradually taken apart all the laboriously constructed works. Nothing remains but boards and splinters, rusted anchor bolts and loops of telephone wire strewn across the trail.

Facing the next 100 feet of the mountain, John and I arranged the length of rope so that we were connected, and delicately worked part way up the cold and ice-streaked cliff. Halfway to the top we came to even more ice, too much ice, thick and treacherous ice. A pause. Cold, stiff, hungry and tired, we decided to give it up, try another day when the sun shone and little birds came out to sing. Taking turns—one descending while the other looped the rope around a rock—we belayed each other back down the bleak face, reencountered the yellow dog at the base of the cliff, and marched down the trail to camp and truck, defeated but looking forward to food and drink.

Next day the weather changed, the temperatures soared, the snow and ice began to melt. A week later I returned to Baboquivari and scrambled easily to the peak, standing where William O. Douglas had stood years earlier, and looking out over the desert.

The view from the peak is good, if not always perfect. When I was there I could see about half of southern Arizona and quite a parcel of Mexican Sonora and a lot of mountains: the Santa Catalinas, the Ajos, the Huachucas, the Agua Dulces, and the Pinacates and others down in Mexico. When the air is clear, I've been told, you can see the waters of the Gulf of California, some 150 miles away by line of sight. Unfortunately the air is seldom clear in Arizona any more and on that day I could not see the gulf.

Nearby on the peak was the scattered wreckage of the lookout shack, never used for anything but shelter for a generation of hikers and climbers, and now virtually demolished. In an ammunition box cached in the rocks near the ruined shack was a register book, which I signed, and where, as I ate some cheese and rested a while, I read the inscriptions and inspirations of previous signers.

Something about climbing a mountain, even a modest one like Baboquivari, brings out the poet, the exhibitionist or the clown in every man, woman and child. In this register book, for example, were several notations by a woman who called herself "the third best lady mountain climber in the state of Arizona." There was one by "the best 12-year-old climber in the Southwest." Someone wrote, "Easter Sunday: We did it for Jesus." There were the signatures of my friends John and Joanna McComb, who have climbed this peak, from all sides, more than 20 times each. And then there were several pages of sermonizing by some Mormon missionaries who had taken time off from their labors in the Papago Reservation to come climb this heathen peak. The sermons were followed by one line from Pete Cowgill, Arizona journalist: "Don't preach to me on mountaintops."

Okay, I thought, Amen, I'll go along with that. No more preaching on mountaintops. I closed the book. I finished my cheese. I relaced my boots and ate some snow and descended the mountain.

Dreams of Desert Treasure

In her desert classic, *The Land of Little Rain,* Mary Austin remarked on "the palpable sense of mystery in the desert air" that "breeds fables, chiefly of lost treasure." In the mountains of the Sonoran Desert, rumors of treasure contained some truth. Beginning before the Civil War and for more than 50 years—until copper became more prized than gold and silver—the Arizona hills echoed to the sound of the prospector's pick and the bray of his burro.

In the late 1850s news of gold on the Gila River drew thousands of fortune seekers, usually lone operators. The lucky ones found gold in river beds or in surface gravel, and usually extracted it by panning: the prospector would wash loose sand and pebbles from a panful of dirt, leaving the heavier rock to be sifted for nuggets of gold.

These surface deposits were all too quickly depleted. In 1858 prospectors at Gila City, site of the first gold rush, gathered as much as $100 in gold a day, but by 1864 "the color had played out," as the prospectors put it, and the town had dwindled, in the words of one observer, to "three chimneys and a coyote."

Mining for silver was more complicated: ore usually had to be hacked out of the rock and processed. By the mid-1870s hard-rock silver-mining operations had begun on a large scale in the Pinal Mountains north of Tucson. Most of the solitary prospectors gave way to small mining companies that hired gangs of men. Towns that started as a few shacks grew helter-skelter as increasing numbers of workers arrived, many with families. The smell of wealth—and the miners' need for food, drink and entertainment—attracted not only ranchers and farmers but gamblers and saloonkeepers.

Yet few of the miners and their hangers-on were really interested in settling. They came to get what they could from the land and then moved on. Most of the hastily built towns were abandoned. With the demonetization of silver in 1893 and the new-found importance of copper to the burgeoning electrical industry, dreams of riches in the desert became harder and harder for small entrepreneurs to realize. After the first decade of the 20th Century, the entrances of forsaken mines were, for the most part, left to the lizards.

Photographed around 1900, this prospector was one of the last of a breed of desert treasure seekers. His tough, sure-footed mules tended to be ornery like the burros—called Arizona nightingales for their high-pitched bray—favored by many prospectors. One contrary burro is even credited with helping to discover the richest gold deposit in Arizona: the Vulture Mine at Wickenberg. In a rage when the beast refused to be caught, its master pelted it with rocks—which fell far short of their target because they were so heavy with gold.

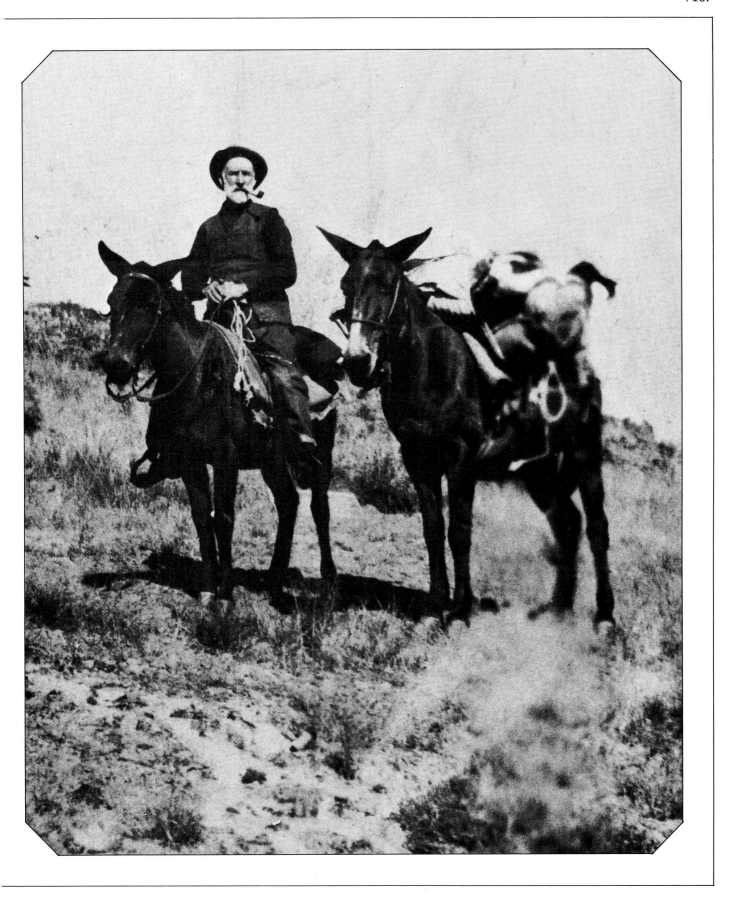

Hard-rock silver miners of the 1890s gather outside a tunnel entrance to the Gunsight Mine. A child—evidently too young for work, though children often toiled beside the grownups to augment family income—perches on a narrow-gauge railway truck used to haul ore from the mine tunnel.

On a steep cliffside, workers pause momentarily on the rocky path leading to a mine entrance. The buildings at upper left were storage sheds and living quarters. The long, sloping structure at lower left was used to funnel ore down the mountainside to trains that hauled it to the smelter.

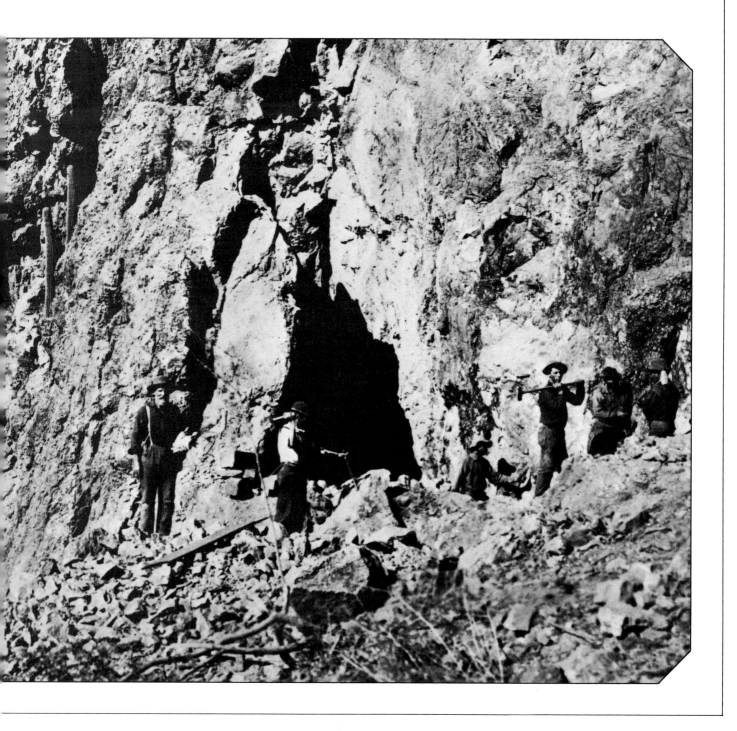

110/

Beams for shoring up tunnels lie in long stacks at the Silver King Mine in the Pinal Mountains. Hauled in by teams of mules and burros, a supply of timber was vital to mine operations because the excavated tunnels often contained large quantities of loose rock. To prevent cave-ins, the beams were placed along the sides and ceilings of the tunnels.

5/ Wild Palms and Gold Mines

*...there is a special kind of beauty for every hour
the mountain knows, beauty which man perceives without
participating, beauty to which he feels himself a stranger.*

MARY AUSTIN/ *THE LAND OF JOURNEYS' ENDING*

Approaching the Kofa Mountains from the west, off Highway 95 in southwest Arizona, you see gaunt burned porphyritic cliffs rising from the desert plain like fortifications for a race of giants. Half buried in their own eroded debris, they look much older than the human imagination can comprehend, apocryphal, legendary.

They glow, these mountains, as if with an inner fire. The effect is caused by the coloration of the rock and its almost total nakedness. In one of the driest parts of a dry region, the Kofas support only the sparsest vegetation—brittlebush (blooming bright and yellow in January) teddy bear cholla and very hairy prickly pear, cotton-top mini-headed barrel cactus with its bloodshot-pink hooked barbs, here and there a mesquite or ironwood, an occasional creosote. And each plant is well separated from its neighbor, rationing not light nor space but water.

The aridity, even in midwinter, sucks at the pores of your flesh, dries the sweat as fast as it emerges from your skin, keeps you cool, dehydrates you mighty quick unless you keep gulping down water. Water, water, water. . . . You look for it everywhere you go, out here. Nothing so marvelous, so rapturous, so miraculous as water in the desert.

The dirt road winding eastward from Highway 95 leads toward a dark gap in the west façade of the Kofas. Huge buttresses of andesite and metamorphosed volcanic tuff stand on either side of the gap, which is actually the mouth of Palm Canyon. Beyond and above the gap are more tiers and terraces of rust-colored stone, surmounted by the 4,877-foot-high mesa called Signal Peak. A brutal hulk of rock, it looks like a titanic altar, rotten and corroded with the blood of gods. Like mangled iron from some cosmic collision. Or like the crumbling ruin of a Castilian castle. No, this is all poetical rubbish. The mountain looks like what it is, the eroded remnants of igneous intrusions, volcanic rubble, ash and cinder and sediment. Which is enough.

Kofa is an acronym for King of Arizona, which in turn is the name of a gold mine, no longer operated, down on the southwest flank of the range. The original name for the Kofas was the S.H. Mountains. According to one story, early prospectors named the range S.H. because of prominent quadrangular rock formations near the summit that resemble old-fashioned outhouses. Later, out of courtesy to pioneer ladies, S.H. was interpreted to mean Short Horn instead of the real, but unmentionable, name. Government map makers settled the controversy in their characteristic Bowdlerian fashion by choosing the present official name, although the original initials can still be seen on the earliest Geological Survey maps.

As in the Superstition Mountains, the Kofas have attracted more than a proportionate share of fortune hunters, gold seekers, those who come to search for whatever it is they lost a long time ago. We, on the other hand, have come to see the wild palm trees, the California fan palms, *Washingtonia filifera,* which grow in various oases in southern California and Baja California, and in only a few areas in Arizona, the northernmost and easternmost limit of their range.

Nine miles of dust and gravel bring us to a dead end, a sort of parking lot bulldozed out of the side of a slope, where the trail into Palm Canyon begins. We are now in what is called the Kofa National Wildlife Refuge, an extensive portion of public real estate administered by the U.S. Fish and Wildlife Service, Department of the Interior.

A wildlife sanctuary, the Kofas were opened in 1955 to hunting on a restricted basis, a move that sizably increased the revenues of the Arizona Game and Fish Department through the sale of licenses. The principal attraction here for hunters is the desert bighorn sheep, and perhaps now is the right time and place to say what must be said about trophy hunters:

I am not against hunters or hunting. Many of us who call ourselves conservationists or wilderness nuts or nature freaks have been hunters too. Born and raised on a Pennsylvania farm, I spent much of my boyhood in the pursuit and slaughter of small mammals. I was a trapper and familiar with the sight of a muskrat frozen in ice or the look of a gnawed-off fox's leg in the steel jaws of one of my Victor traps. As a boy such things troubled me only slightly. I thought nothing of killing rabbits, squirrels and ringneck pheasants for the table, and badgers, groundhogs and skunks for sport. We were helping to rid the world of "varmints"—an honorable undertaking.

Later, in the Southwest, in the glory of youth, I became an avid deer-slayer, often by jack light under the stars, often the day before the season opened (hiding my kill in the woods for 24 hours), and sometimes even fair, square and legally. I didn't care. It was all for the sake of putting meat on the table and deerskin gloves on my sweetheart's hands. Honorable work, nothing a man need be ashamed of.

But I discovered gradually that I no longer found much pleasure in killing for the sake of killing. The more I hunted the more I found it necessary to justify my activity by convincing myself that I was doing it for the sake of the meat. I could no longer kill anything I did not intend to eat. Why? Over a period of years the answer came to me: I was growing up. Even the meat was only a pretext, I realized, not a genuine need. There were others whose need for venison was far greater than

Signal Peak

mine: Indians, for example, and out-of-work copper miners, and students and Mexicans living a submarginal existence. And mountain lions. Yes, most especially the lions, for whom deer meat is basic, the staple of their diet. (And who needs lions? We all do—including the deer. Most especially the deer. For their own evolutionary good.)

Therefore I gave up even the annual deer hunt. Not however on absolute moral grounds—please note that. When and if I ever need the meat I shall load up the old .30-30 and go trudging off again into the mountain dawn. As for all my friends and countrymen who continue to hunt deer, or anything else that is good to eat, in plentiful supply, in no danger of extinction, I say *buena cacería*—good hunting. I see nothing wrong in it; I perceive no moral superiority in the position of the ethical vegetarian who exploits cattle and goats for their milk, uproots harmless carrots, mutilates innocent turnips, violates cabbages and plunders fruit trees to keep body and soul conjoined. All must eat to survive; all must kill in order to eat. The system demands it and our only moral obligation under this system is to do what killing we must in the proper spirit of humility, gratitude and grace.

Trophy hunting, however, is another matter, one that lacks the most

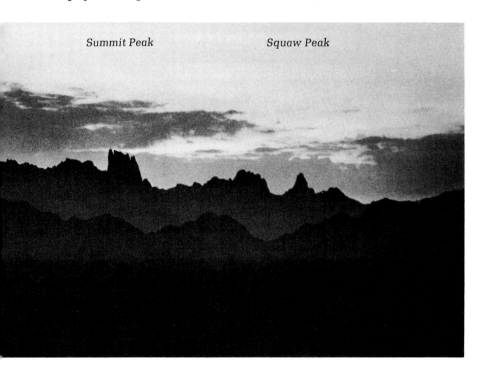

Summit Peak   Squaw Peak

Sharply outlined against the sunset, the jagged crest of the Kofa Mountains in southwest Arizona resembles the skyline of a primitive metropolis of palaces and turrets. The range, whose principal peaks are identified in the picture, is volcanic in origin, and covered with a layer of lava that is 2,000 feet thick in places. The discovery of veins of ore-bearing rock around the turn of the century set off a flurry of gold and silver mining and also won the Kofas their name, after the King of Arizona, a gold mine abandoned in 1910. Today the mountains are best known as a refuge for bighorn sheep.

elementary justification. Hunters do not kill bighorn sheep or mountain lions or javelinas because they need the meat. (Which is not to say that these animals cannot be eaten if the need arises.) Nor can anyone honestly claim to kill such animals in self-defense; none of them are ever likely to attack humans, unless cornered or molested. The only reason these animals are still subject to hunting is because some men—not many—find a weird sort of psychological gratification in the slaughter of them. It does not even appear to be a question of establishing a sense of manhood through the killing, because other more legitimate game, deer for example, are amply available. The purpose of trophy hunting seems to be no more than the collection of heads for the sake of the heads. It is a hobby then, admittedly one sometimes involving skill and always great expense of time and money, pursued with the passion other men reserve for the pursuit of women, gold, power or fame.

Bighorn sheep have become particular victims of this head-hunting mania. Among the collectors of sheep heads there is a magical achievement called the Grand Slam—which means the killing of one full-grown ram from each of four distinct kinds of wild sheep found on the North American continent. The four are the desert bighorn, the Rocky Mountain bighorn, the Stone sheep and the Dall. If you can kill all four you have hit a Grand Slam—a homer with the bases loaded. Four stuffed sheep heads to mount on your rumpus-room wall.

Perhaps none of this would matter much if bighorns (and lions and javelinas et al.) were as common as jack rabbits and mule deer. So long as the animal kingdom can bear it, the peculiar hobbies of trophy hunters would get no argument from me. The harm lies in the fact that they hunt most eagerly the very animals that are most in danger of extinction, such as polar bears, leopards, jaguars, grizzly bears and ibexes, as well as the North American bighorn sheep. It appears that the very rarity of an animal makes its dead head all the more desirable.

True, the desert bighorn is protected by law. The hunting of it is severely regulated, with only a limited number of permits issued each year. In theory, at least, the bighorn population should be sustained. Unfortunately a considerable amount of poaching goes on, most of it by wealthy hunters who fail to obtain one of the much-prized official permits, then pay exorbitant fees to unscrupulous professional guides and willingly risk a fine if caught. Luxury poaching has become so common, as the bighorn become harder and harder to find, that one guide announced he was quitting the business altogether rather than participate any longer in the extermination of a species.

Other more significant factors contribute to the decline of the desert bighorn. Among these are parasites, disease and stress, as well as the loss of habitat. Of course we do not fully know what afflictions plagued the bighorn years ago before the westward migration of that breed known as the American. But with the pioneers came domestic livestock and their parasites. *Psoroptes* mites cause scabies by burrowing under the skin and creating scabs; these take sections of skin with them when they eventually fall off. Botflies induce sinusitis, depositing eggs in the sheeps' nostrils. The botfly larvae may hatch in any of hundreds of small, interconnecting nasal cavities from which they cannot escape; when the larvae die, infection results. Like scabies, sinusitis often weakens the animal to the point where it contracts pneumonia and dies.

Almost any kind of strange noise or other disturbance leads to stress in bighorns, making them vulnerable to disease. Hordes of nature lovers (such as myself) invade their sanctuaries. Noisy aircraft disturb their privacy. The military's use of much of the Southwest as a bombing and gunnery range may be producing deleterious if not precisely known effects upon the stability of the species. And most serious of all, interstate highways and the fences around cattle ranches obstruct the free migration of the bighorn herds from one mountain range to another when their feed or water conditions require a change of location.

Competition with man and his livestock has taken its toll on the desert bighorn. Nevertheless they may yet be saved. All of the things conducive to a good life for the bighorn are now present in the Kofa National Wildlife Refuge. In fact, the bighorn population there has increased to the extent that in some years the refuge officials have had to move 20 to 30 sheep to other areas of Arizona where the count is low.

Back to the wild palms of the Kofas. Leaving our jeep, the two of us walked a well-beaten trail into the mouth of Palm Canyon and followed it up a wash until we could see the first group of palms. They grow in a deep, narrow side canyon, high up a steep pitch. There is no water visible on the surface, so that the area does not resemble what we think of as an oasis, but there is evidently enough water trickling through the rock just below the surface to keep the palms thriving. Some of these palms are 30 feet tall, but because of the mountainous terrain they appear, from a distance, much smaller. The dangling dead fronds of the trees form a thatch about the trunks, very dry and flammable. One group of palms seemed to have been set on fire in the recent past, probably by man, for the trunks were completely blackened. The trees were

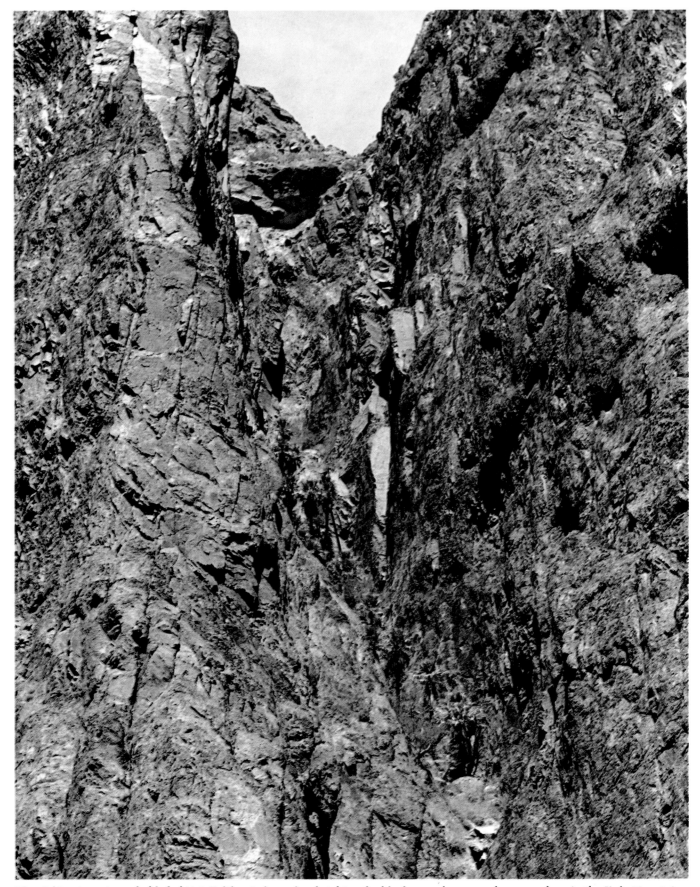

Flourishing in an improbable habitat, California fan palms brighten the bleakness of a cragged canyon deep in the Kofa Mountains.

alive, however, green and flourishing above the fire line. According to Peggy Larson in her book *Deserts of America,* the palms not only are able to survive an occasional fire but may even benefit from it; fire clears away the underbrush surrounding the palms, giving the young seedlings an opportunity for unobstructed growth. Destruction of competing shrubs also leaves more water for the fire-resistant trees.

The idea that fire plays a beneficial as well as inevitable part in the growth and regeneration of trees is rapidly gaining acceptance among professional foresters; what is good for wild palms may also be good for the ponderosa, the spruce, the fir and the aspen. After all, as is readily apparent to common sense, both lightning and great forests have been around for a long time, and the forests have survived.

These Arizona wild palms do not produce dates, but they do produce a fruit that used to be eaten by the desert Indians. Botanists guess that an individual palm lives from 150 to 200 years, and in favored locations —not in the inhospitable Kofa Mountains—will grow as tall as 50 feet. The annual crop of seeds remains dormant until temperature and moisture conditions are suitable. Where palms and water are present in ample number and quantity, a special kind of plant and animal community is formed, essentially different in character from the surrounding desert; this ecologists term a micro-habitat—the oasis.

We walked farther up Palm Canyon, climbing steadily toward the sunlit ramparts beyond. On the way we saw more palms, some in groups, some alone, but almost always—we saw only one exception—growing on the sunny, south-facing side of the canyon. The canyon was very silent that evening; we saw or heard no sign of animal life except now and then a little gray bird flitting through the brush.

It might have been wiser, so late in the day, to turn back to our jeep and make camp. Instead, under the spell of the mountain and the desire for the new, we continued scrambling up the narrow canyon, climbing over and around boulders and up little scarps of bedrock, until finally we emerged from the canyon to find ourselves in a basin a mile wide, walled in by more cliffs on the east and south. To the north we could see a notch or pass in the surrounding wall. Traversing the steep talus slope of loose rock, richly studded with teddy bear cholla, we made our way toward the opening.

Teddy bear cholla, *Opuntia bigelovii,* makes a formidable obstacle in rough terrain. A shrubby sort of cactus, usually growing no more than four feet high, it is so densely covered with inch-long silvery-golden

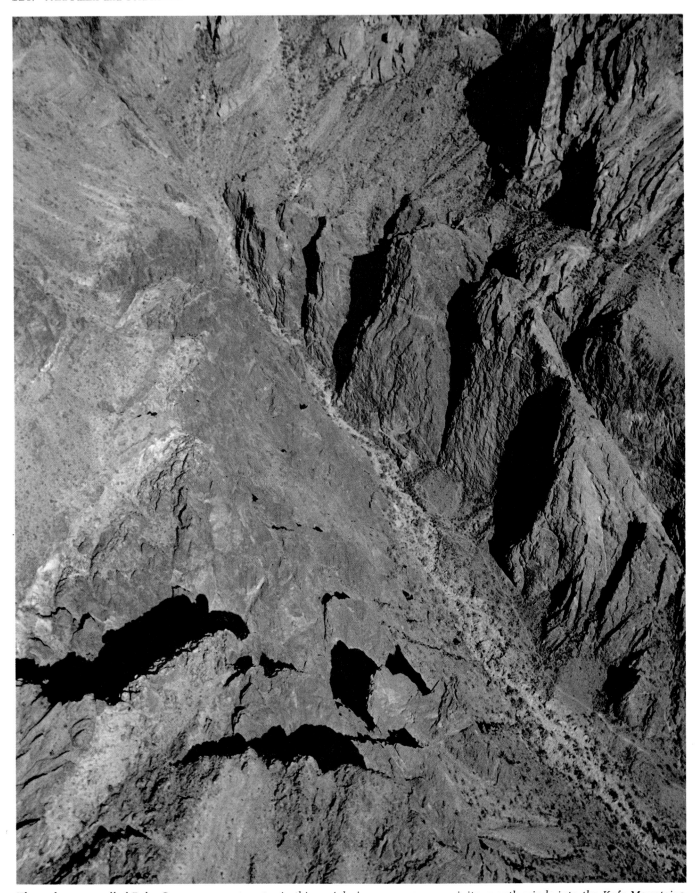

Through steep-walled Palm Canyon, seen at center in this aerial view, a narrow, precipitous path winds into the Kofa Mountains.

spines that from a distance it presents a soft, furry aspect. Thus the common name. But this plant is anything but cuddly. The spines are attached to stubby joints of woody material, and the slightest contact is enough to remove an entire joint—easily detachable from the branches—and hang it on your skin. Once attached to skin or clothing, the joint is not easily removed; if you try to pluck it off with your hand, the joint just transfers its allegiance to the hand, giving you a palmful of spines. The usual solution is to brush the joint away with a pair of sticks or stones; then you pluck out the spines, one by one, from your flesh or clothing. But perhaps the best approach is simply to slide a comb under the joint and lift. This takes care of the whole thing at once.

A half hour's scramble brought us to the pass on the north. From there we could see what looked like a fairly easy descent, down a long sloping shelf of rock, to the desert floor a couple of thousand feet below. The sun was already hovering on the horizon and a decision had to be made quickly: to return the way we had come, a long but certain route, or take a chance on what looked to be a much faster way down, but one that might hold difficulties not visible from above.

We elected to gamble. Equipping ourselves with dead agave stalks for balance and support in the brush and scree, we started down. For a while, as the darkness settled in, all went well. The route was clear, lessening the danger of a sprained ankle or a fall on the head. We came across a half dozen young fan palms growing in a secluded place, hiding from the world, from us tourists. We found a sheep trail and piles of mahogany-colored pellets at lookout and resting places; examining the droppings, breaking them open, I guessed that they might have been a month old. So the sheep were still around—somewhere. Watching us, perhaps; bighorns are notoriously curious, like cats. Which often proves to be their undoing. But they were all out of sight. Or maybe they had left the Kofas for the Castle Dome Mountains, across Stagecoach Pass and King Valley to the south. Or maybe they had moved northward into the New Water Mountains.

In the lavender gloom, rapidly thickening to night, we approached the foot of the mountain. Here we discovered that our sloping shelf terminated in a series of deep, narrow canyons quite inaccessible from above. We seemed to be rimmed up, trapped in a place where further descent was impossible. If we had had 200 feet of rope with us we might have been able to rappel down into the canyons. But we had no rope.

We began thinking about gathering wood and starting a fire. It would be a tedious cold night, on this desert mountain in January, with nothing to protect us from the weather but our clothes and maybe a cave in the rock if we could find one. Wandering about on that rocky promontory, the shadowy depths on either side, I found a little niche in the rim and a rubble-filled channel leading down. The way out? We took it, proceeding cautiously, and discovered with pleasure that the route did indeed go clear to the bottom of one of the side canyons below.

Fighting our way through the thorny brush, stumbling over loose and unbalanced rocks, we finally reached the solid rock of the canyon floor. Here we came upon a series of three shapely water-filled natural tanks in the stone, each about three times the size and depth of a conventional bathtub. By this time we were thirsty as well as tired, hungry and a bit worried; we named the pools Salvation Tanks. There are many such tanks—some a lot larger—in these otherwise barren mountains: scoured by the rare but powerful summer floods, they will retain water for days, sometimes weeks or months, wherever the depth is great enough and the shade adequate to prevent rapid evaporation.

We drank our fill of the cool, stagnant but potable water, then worked our way out of the canyon and around the base of the mountain, another three or four miles, to the road and the jeep. Under a sky all dazzling with stars and sliding meteors—there seemed to be a shower of them that night—we built a fire and made our supper of bacon and beans, then bedded down in the welcome luxury of old Army surplus mummy bags for a good and well-earned winter night's sleep.

The next day we went forth to inspect some of the old-time gold mines in the foothills of the Kofas. Back to the highway, south, east on a dirt road through King Valley and north at Zero Zero Junction brought us after 20 miles of hard, rocky, dusty jeepherding to a group of abandoned mines: the King of Arizona, the Rob Roy and the North Star.

The remains consisted of a few old weatherbeaten shacks, the ruins of many more, a scattering of ancient rusted mining machinery, and on the hillsides the mine entrances and the huge gray tailing dumps. I should not say that these mines have been completely abandoned; although none have been in operation for many years, they do remain private property and active mining claims have been staked out around each. Both the King of Arizona Mine and the North Star Mine are protected by resident caretakers.

Neither mine looks like much now, since they have been picked over for so long by rock hounds and souvenir hunters. But the King of Ar-

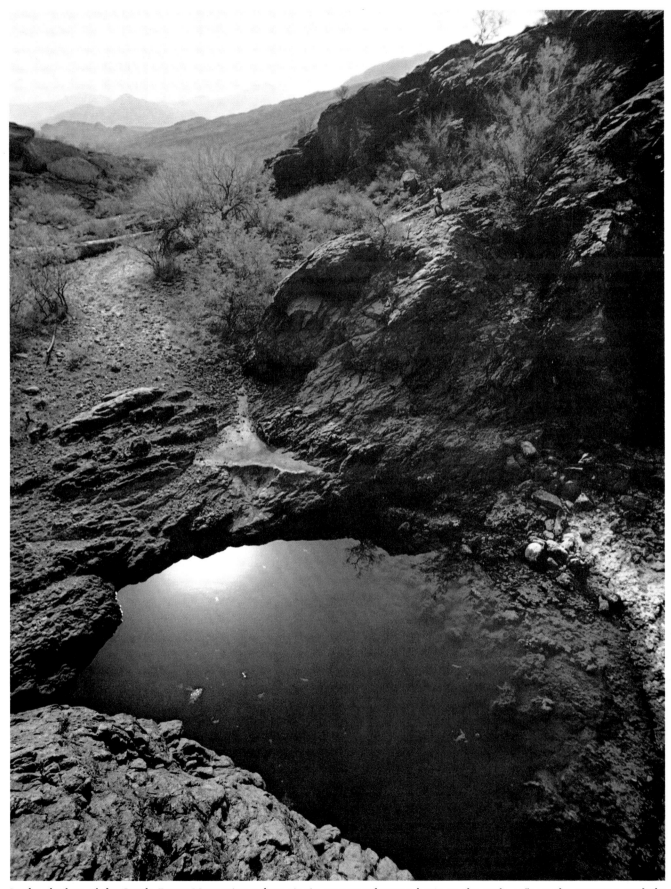

In the shadow of the Castle Dome Mountains a deep tinaja, or natural water basin in the rock, reflects the morning sunlight.

izona, discovered in 1896 by one Charles E. Eichelberger, is supposed to have produced three and a half million dollars' worth of gold from 1897 until 1910, by which time the vein was worked out. The ore was milled near the mine by what is called the amalgamation process, with cyanide treatment added later, both methods requiring much water. Water was a serious problem in this barren area, but the miners solved it by drilling deep wells nearby, where the water was pumped out with power supplied through a wood-burning boiler plant. This pumping system consumed so much firewood that the land for miles around was largely stripped of mesquite and ironwood, the only fuels available.

Even today, more than seven decades after the operation was discontinued, these trees are still uncommon among the foothills on the south side of the Kofa Mountains. But one well the miners dug was a good one; still in use, it supplies the domestic needs of the half dozen individuals who now live in the area. The milling job was also very thorough; according to the caretaker whom I interviewed on the site, the gold ore from this mine was crushed, amalgamated and acid-treated so completely that no one has ever succeeded in attempts to rework the tailings—even though in most other places, with improved methods of refining ore, miners have found the tailing dumps of old silver and gold mines to be one of the most valuable sources of those precious metals.

Two miles north of the King of Arizona is what remains of the North Star Mine, another allegedly fabulous producer. (Some regional historians believe that the production of these old mines was greatly exaggerated at the time by their owners, for the purpose of luring more investment capital.) Like the King of Arizona, the North Star is largely a ruin now; a great deal of the machinery and iron rails has been removed by commercial scavengers. The mine is said to have produced a little over a million dollars' worth of gold ore. This figure refers of course to the gross value of the production; costs were so high in mining and milling in this remote and nearly waterless location that the net profits were probably not great, if there were any at all. By 1911, one year after the King of Arizona was closed down, the North Star too reached its "economic limits"—meaning that miners and geologists believed more gold was present, but that current prices were not high enough to justify the expenditures that would be required to recover the ore. This is the principal reason spokesmen for the mining industries had frequently pressured Congress to raise government prices for gold and silver; in effect they asked for public subsidies to make it profitable for them to extract these metals from the ground. From *public* ground, by the way: most mining in the West takes place in what are supposed to be public lands, presumably the property of all Americans.

There was once a spell of fine romance attached to prospecting and mining, especially in the realm of gold, as anyone will testify who has read such books as J. Frank Dobie's *Apache Gold and Yaqui Silver,* or that marvelous novel by B. Traven, *The Treasure of the Sierra Madre.* But the romantic period in metal and mineral extraction has long since passed. The eccentric and fiercely individualistic types who worked alone, towing a burro over the hills, are mostly gone; the legendary Seldom Seen Slim of Death Valley, for example, will never be seen again—he died some years ago.

Today almost all serious prospecting is carried out by teams of college-trained geologists on the payroll of giant world-girdling corporations such as Kennecott and Anaconda. Some time is spent seeking out gold and silver, but today's prospectors are after things more basic: copper, zinc, iron, manganese, coal, oil shale, sand tars, molybdenum, titanium, uranium. When they locate something salable they will butcher whole mountains to remove it from the earth.

Fortunately no such dismal fate has yet overtaken the ancient stony battlements of the Kofas. As we discovered in two more days of exploration, this range still remains essentially undamaged by man or his works. Perhaps it cannot be considered pristine wilderness, because trails, jeep roads and mining ruins are many, but it surely belongs in the category called primitive. What these mountains really need from us is to be mostly left alone, neither exploited nor—perhaps equally dangerous in the long run—loved to death. That the sheep may safely graze. That the lion may lie down with the lamb. (In order to eat it.) That islands of relative peace, order and sanity may remain amidst the chaos of a mindless industrialism. Tranquility, I reckon, like water or money or seed corn, can usefully be stored away in safe places.

The Water Misers

ILLUSTRATED BY BARRY DRISCOLL

Much of the Sonoran Desert averages less than 10 inches of rain a year, but despite the aridity some wildlife manages to survive—and even thrive—there. The species that succeed are those that have found ways to cope with the long periods of drought, employing a variety of mechanisms to ensure the fullest use of the water available to them, venturing onto the desert floor only after the sapping sun has set, and in general husbanding their energies.

Among the animals that have adapted to desert life, eight of the most intriguing appear on the following pages in paintings by the eminent British wildlife artist Barry Driscoll, based on his researches both in the field and at the Arizona-Sonora Desert Museum near Tucson. Perhaps fittingly, the portrait gallery begins with the kangaroo rat (right), which its admirers acclaim as "the rodent that never drinks water." This diminutive creature—three inches of body and seven inches of tail—is totally geared to conserving liquid.

The kangaroo rat has no sweat glands; it cools off by breathing. Moreover, its nasal passages are at a lower temperature than the rest of its body: as warm exhalations travel through the passages, some moisture condenses and is retained by the animal. Another built-in aid to survival is the kangaroo rat's kidneys, among the most efficient possessed by any mammal. Although all animals flush out uric wastes with water, this rat rarely urinates. It can concentrate its uric wastes until they are less a fluid than a kind of paste. Therefore, the amount of water expended is very small.

Diet and habitat also help the kangaroo rat combat the desert's dehydrating effects. Its primary source of nourishment is the carbohydrate in dry seeds. Although these contain only 4 per cent water, the animal metabolizes moisture as well as energy from the seed particles.

Its burrow provides added insurance. The rat digs it deep enough so that a year-round temperature between 46° F. and 85° F.—and a relative humidity between 30 and 50 per cent—is maintained, especially when the occupant plugs the burrow entrance with dirt.

The beneficent protections that nature has afforded the kangaroo rat seem nothing less than a marvel. But it is one that is matched in the cases of the seven other creatures portrayed, each with remarkable survival techniques of its own.

As agile as the large mammal for which it is named, the kangaroo rat is well protected not only against desert dryness but also against the host of predators that find it a tempting tidbit. Using its oversized hind legs and a bipedal form of locomotion (most rodents run on all four legs), it can leap almost two feet in any direction, including straight up, and execute mid-air pivots. The rat's huge inner ears and long tufted tail help provide the balance such acrobatics require.

The Case for a Much Maligned Reptile

Endowed with a stubby low-slung body, which measures about a foot and a half long at maturity, and a rough, irregularly patterned skin, the Gila monster is the most fearsome-looking member of the desert animal kingdom.

For all its dire aspect, which has led to the widely held notion that this lizard is lethal to man, the Gila monster is too sluggish and timid to offer a real threat to humans. True, it is one of the world's only two poisonous lizards (the other is a relative, the Mexican beaded lizard), but the Gila rarely unleashes the painful venom secreted by glands in its lower jaw. Unlike the rattlesnake, which may strike with minimal warning at the unwary passerby, the Gila avoids man and rarely bites unless handled or otherwise provoked—holding on bulldog fashion and grinding with its powerful jaws. It uses its venom primarily to stun the other reptiles and birds whose eggs constitute much of its normal diet and provide both the protein and fluids it needs. Even so, the Gila rarely fights for its food, invariably retreating from danger.

In the seasons when other animals are busy laying eggs, this lizard emerges to conduct solitary hunting forays. In winter it snuggles into a humid burrow in a state of decreased metabolism, drawing on fat stored in its tail. Thus the Gila spends part of its life in a stupor, a shy, inoffensive creature that belies the malevolent myths surrounding it.

A Gregarious Desert Pig

A distant kin of the domestic swine and the European wild boar, the collared peccary, or javelina, can grow as big as a fox hound. A social animal, it protects itself against predators by traveling in groups.

An essential—but little understood—means of communication between members of a group of these animals is a musk gland, located on the javelina's hindquarters and exposed by raising its bristles (*far left*). A pungent odor exuded by the gland may serve individuals within the group as a means of asserting their dominance; but some biologists also think the whole group may use the smell to stake out its collective territory in the desert—warning other javelinas not to encroach.

A bunch of javelinas—about a dozen in all—will wander ceaselessly through cactus country scrubland to appease their prodigious appetites. The animal's favored foods are cactus and roots, which it is able to shovel up by means of its sizable snout. In times of drought, when water holes evaporate, its diet of cholla and prickly-pear cactus provides water as well as food. Consuming these spiny plants poses no problem for the javelina. It can mouth a pad of cactus to blunt the largest spines; then, ignoring the smaller spines, it gobbles the pulp.

If javelinas sense the presence of potential danger from animals or humans, the herd may charge, but more often it will flee.

A Nimble and Resourceful Bird

Pioneers crossing the Sonoran Desert in the late 19th Century often found an odd two-foot-long bird trotting tirelessly on the ground beside their wagon wheels. They dubbed this seemingly earthbound creature the roadrunner.

Actually, the roadrunner can take to the air if necessary, but it prefers to jog on "X"-shaped clawed feet that provide traction on the desert sand. It is capable of going as fast as 15 miles per hour and uses its foot-long tail as a combination rudder and flap, swiveling it in order to change course or raising it upright, like a feathered exclamation point, in order to come to a stop.

Unlike many desert birds, the roadrunner does not migrate during dry seasons, depending for fluids on its omnivorous diet—which even includes small rattlesnakes. One delightful cactus country legend has it that the bird fences in a sleeping rattler with the prickly joints of the cholla cactus; upon awakening, so the story goes, the snake, finding itself hopelessly ensnared by spines, bites itself to death.

A real confrontation between a roadrunner and a rattler is dramatic enough. Relying on its great ability to move nimbly, the bird dances about the rattler, which strikes uselessly at the gyrating bird, expending its venom. Then, stunning the rattler with powerful thrusts of its beak, the roadrunner proceeds to stuff the victim down its gullet.

The Incongruous Coatimundi

Encountering a coatimundi is like coming upon a bizarre jigsaw puzzle. The first glimpse is of an apparently disembodied furry brown tail, aimed skyward, bobbing across the horizon. Then the animal comes into full view, and from its long nose to its fluffy banded tail it looks thoroughly implausible: a seeming amalgam of pig, bear cub and raccoon.

This creature, called the coati *(ko-AH-tee)* for short—and known locally to Arizonans as the chulu—is a tropical relative of the raccoon; the coati drifted from South and Central America north to the mountains dotting the cactus country. It is an omnivorous feeder and a skilled climber, scaling trees to doze both night and day. In the cooler hours of dawn and dusk it descends to forage for meals, which, depending on the time of year and its own prowess, range from small rodents and lizards to berries and roots.

Like javelinas, coatis band together for survival, segregating themselves by sex, with the mature males in groups separate from the females and their offspring. But despite the safety they seek in numbers, some coatimundis have a baffling reaction to danger. Agile and comfortable in the trees, which would usually be their safest refuge, they will jump to the ground when threatened and take to their heels across country —where they are capable of surprising speed but are no match for a hungry bobcat.

A Sturdy, Retiring Turtle

For nine months of the year, the desert tortoise hoards liquids like a miser pinching pennies, storing water in a bladder inside its upper shell; next to the kangaroo rat it is the desert's best conserver of moisture. Like the kangaroo rat, it concentrates uric wastes to conserve vital body fluids, though unlike the kangaroo rat it will drink its fill of water when it gets the chance. Between drinks, its leathery skin and hard shell help keep evaporation loss to a minimum.

During dry seasons the desert tortoise retreats to a cool, moist den and stays put there for the better part of the day, subsisting on a diet of herbs and grasses. It livens up only in the summer rainy season, when succulent annuals in bloom and frequent rain pools tempt it out of its den to feast and drink.

It also mates at this time, a process often preceded by jousts between rival males. After some nipping, the contenders begin to ram each other with shovellike extensions of the lower shell. The goal is to immobilize the opponent by flipping it over on its back.

In this species of turtle growth is slow; a mature desert tortoise measures about nine inches long. The model for the 13-inch specimen shown here was perhaps 25 years old, and is in museum captivity. Had it been left to live in the desert, its tough carapace would have been scarred from digging burrows in the rocky desert soil.

The Snake with a Telltale Signature

Parallel slash marks in the sand lead across the dunes and end abruptly in a circle. Inside it lies what from a slight distance appears to be a coil of rope: it is the Sonora sidewinder, lurking in ambush.

One of the smaller of the rattlesnakes, averaging only about 18 inches long, the sidewinder is named for its unique shimmying movement. It travels across the desert by hurling itself forward obliquely, looping its body in successive "S" curves. This rapid, sinuous movement produces the snake's distinctive trademark: a series of separate straight lines, each one ending in a "J" curve made by the snake's neck and head, with the curve sweeping in the direction of the snake's forward progress.

The sidewinder hunts only when the sun is down, preying on lizards, kangaroo rats and other rodents, and utilizing a set of highly efficient hunting tools: a mottled buff skin ideal for desert camouflage; two pits located on each side of the head, which sense heat from nearby bodies; a forked tongue that picks up even the faintest odors; and a fast-working venom—injected through the snake's one-quarter- to one-half-inch-long fangs—that weakens the coagulants in the victim's blood and causes fatal hemorrhage.

Once it has caught the prey, the sidewinder swallows it whole. The victim is reduced by the snake's strong internal acids and absorbed as both food and water.

A High-Speed Quick-Change Artist

The antelope jack rabbit has made its own superb adaptations to desert life. It can speed across its open habitat at 35 miles an hour, bounding along like its namesake and easily outdistancing its predators. Lacking sweat glands, it keeps cool through the unusual means of its eight-inch-long ears: arteries carry blood saturated with body heat to the ears, from which the heat is then dissipated into the air. But this mechanism will work only if the animal spends as much time as possible facing north—a mysterious habit that may enable the rabbit to take advantage of minute temperature differences in air striking its ears from a northerly direction. Whatever the reason, a jack rabbit facing south absorbs heat through its ears.

But perhaps the most fascinating of this animal's adaptations is its ability instantly to turn the color of either one of its flanks from tan to white *(right)*. Called "flashing" and used to befuddle pursuers, this quick change appears when the jack rabbit employs muscles that pull its skin over its flank so as to expose the white underfur.

As it takes off in a full-speed zigzag that a football halfback would envy, the jack rabbit always whitens the side visible to its pursuer. By this maneuver, known as directive coloration, the hare deliberately draws attention to its changes of direction, thereby adding confusion to the chase and aiding its escape.

6/ Down to the Sea of Cortés

---

*No, the desert cannot be fought successfully; and to join it
...one must walk in it. It is then...we gradually find
ourselves in the comforting company of other living and
warm-blooded creatures.*   ANN WOODIN/ HOME IS THE DESERT

From the terrace of my old stone house in the Santa Catalina foothills,
we've been circling outward, farther and farther from the crowded
haunts of Americans, into the wilderness. Each expedition—to the Superstitions, Organ Pipe, Baboquivari, the Kofas—took us a little greater
distance from the cities and from what Thomas Wolfe called "the man-
swarm." And now we come to one of the largest remaining wild areas
in the Sonoran Desert, the northwestern corner of old Mexico where
the desert meets the Gulf of California.

The northern part of this area, called El Gran Desierto on Mexican
maps, includes the great sea of dunes and the numerous volcanic craters and lava flows of the Pinacate region—a place so strange and grand
that it will be an appropriate climax to this exploration of the Sonoran
Desert. But first, in this chapter, we will have a look at the southerly region, the gulf coast and the largely uninhabited desert that bounds it.

As my guide I invited my friend and neighbor Richard Felger, a botanist who has specialized in the ethnobotany—people and plants—of
northwest Sonora. We made our preparations and one January day got
off to an early start at the crack of noon—early for us, anyhow—and
headed south for the border. Avoiding the slow-moving entry at the
city of Nogales, we took a little-traveled dirt road farther to the west
and entered Mexico by way of the village of Sasabe, barely detectable
on the maps, which is one of the nicer things about it.

"Alto," says the road sign by the Mexican border station. We halted, entered the station, obtained our tourist cards and tipped the inspector the customary dollar's worth of pesos. Leaving, I savored those smells characteristic of Mexico—refried beans, burning lard, mesquite and ironwood smoke, wine, manure, hot sheet iron, old adobe baking under the heat of the desert sun.

We drove south by southwest over a rough, rocky, winding dirt road, past mile after mile of burnt adobe brickworks (apparently the chief local industry, after cattle raising), and then into the open desert. Buzzards circled overhead—there always seem to be more buzzards in the sky on the Mexican side of the border. Why? Because both life and death are more abundant down in Mexico. It's the kind of country buzzards love. A candid country, harsh and bare, which is no doubt why it strikes us overcivilized Americans as crude, vulgar and dangerous.

Scrub cattle ranging through the bush galloped off like gnus and wildebeests at our approach. I never saw such weird, scrawny, pied, mottled, humped, long-horned and camel-necked brutes trying to pass as domestic livestock. Most looked like a genetic hash of Hereford, Charolais, Brahman, Angus, moose, ibex, tapir and nightmare. Weaned on cactus, snakeweed and thistle, they showed the gleam of the sun through the translucent barrel of their rib cages. But they could run, they were alive, not only alive but vigorous. I was tempted to think, watching their angular hind ends jouncing away through the dust, that the meat on those critters, if you could find any, might just taste better than the aerated, water-injected, hormone-inflated beef we Americans get from today's semiautomated feed lots in the States.

For most of the afternoon we rambled toward the setting sun through the rolling desert of mesquite, creosote, paloverde and cactus. The saguaros were sparse and stunted-looking; even the prickly pear and cholla do not seem to do too well down here. But the mesquite thrives, growing in dwarf forests over what used to be grassy savanna, according to some ecohistorians. (Overgrazing—the old story.) Every now and then we'd descend into a wash or arroyo where the vegetation was much denser and more varied. Here Felger would stop to beat through the brush, searching for various shrubs and annuals. Some people collect stamps or beer bottles or wagon wheels; professional botanists collect weeds, press them between wooden plates, and store them away in museum files never to be seen by light of day again.

In the evening we paused for an hour to cook our supper on a heap of incandescent ironwood coals. Coyotes wailed the sun down, heavy-footed cattle stumbled through the chaparral, somebody turned on a few stars. We were down in the Mexican desert and pretty pleased with ourselves; it seemed like a retreat through time—of about 50 years.

The January nights are very long and chilly, however, even in Sonora. We drove on to the town of Caborca and put up at a motel beside a stream of freight trucks, buses and California cars rumbling greasily through the gut of the city. This part of Mexico is well assimilated into the industrial-highway culture of North America, and it was without regret that we left it in the blue dawn and headed southwesterly again into the backlands.

Into the backlands, the back of beyond, the original and primitive Mexico. For the next three days we would see very few other human beings and not a motor vehicle of any kind, nor a gas station, nor a telephone pole. On all sides the sun-baked glare of the rock, the dull pallor of the dust, the sunburned trunks of century-old saguaros, the olive drab of mesquite, creosote and ironwood. On the horizon, ancient and crumbling granitic mountains. The inevitable vultures soaring overhead reminded us, though, that somewhere in this brushy wilderness was life, sentient creation, living meat. Hard to see, of course, during the day, for most desert animals keep themselves concealed in the bush or in burrows under the surface of the ground. But you could see their tracks: birds, lizards, rodents, now and then a coyote, here and there the handlike footprints of raccoon, the long claws of badger, the prints of ringtail cat, the heart-shaped hoofmarks of deer and javelina, the rounded pads of bobcat, the more unusual long narrow tracks of chulu.

I have barely begun to name the immense variety of mammals, large and small, that inhabit the desert. There are, for example, dozens of species of little rodents—rock squirrels, pocket gophers, pocket mice, grasshopper mice, cactus mice, kangaroo rats, wood rats, prairie dogs —and a large assortment of skunks, cottontail rabbits, jack rabbits, porcupines, kit foxes and gray foxes.

Some of these animals, especially the rodents and other smaller mammals, may never drink free water in their entire lives. Instead they get by on what moisture they can obtain from plant food and through the internal manufacture of what is called "metabolic water." Particularly distinguished in this regard is the kangaroo rat, which subsists almost entirely on a diet of dried seeds, bathes itself in sand, ignores green and succulent plants, and shuns water even when it is available.

But of all these Sonoran beasts surely the most curious is *Nasua nar-*

Saguaros and salt-tolerant shrubs fringe the dunes that mark the encounter of desert and sea at Desemboque on the Gulf of California.

ica, the chulu, or as it is also called, the coatimundi. Generally chulus travel in bands of a dozen or more, sometimes as many as 200, according to report. But the first one I ever saw was a loner—the older males are often solitary—prowling in a garbage dump near the town of Nogales. Preoccupied with its search for something to eat, the chulu ignored me, or perhaps did not perceive me, and I had ample opportunity to observe it closely.

It was an old one, a grandfather no doubt, unable to keep up with its band, which would also explain why it had been reduced to scavenging in a dump for survival. It was about four feet long, including the two-foot tail, which in the chulu is almost always held upright, at right angles to the body. The fur was rusty brown, the tail marked with light and dark rings like that of a raccoon, which the chulu resembles somewhat. But it looked a little like a small bear, too, with long hind legs and shambling gait. In fact it looked like a mixture of several mammals, with the tail of a raccoon, the gait of a bear, the nose of a pig, a face masked like that of a badger, long wolflike canine teeth, and the lean slab-sided body of a fox or coyote.

As I watched this chulu I saw it turn over rocks, tin cans, boards and other junk with its front paws, exhibiting the manual dexterity of a human. It was probably searching for insects, grubs, arachnids and snakes, as it spent a great deal of time rooting about underneath things with its long and flexible snout. I have learned since that chulus, like coyotes and javelinas, will eat most anything they can find or catch; like us, they are omnivorous.

To see what it would do, I walked toward the chulu, whistled and held out one hand. It looked at me with soft brown eyes, seemingly full of trust, but a snarling grin that exposed long yellow fangs conveyed a different impression. I would not have cared to tangle with this animal barehanded, but before I got close enough to risk attack it turned tail and scurried as nimbly as an old tomcat up the trunk of a big juniper. I left it then in peace.

My favorite desert animal, I think, after such obvious choices as coyote, vulture, cougar, ringtail cat, Gila monster and gopher snake, is the whimsical, cockeyed, half-mad, always eccentric, more or less lovable *Pecari angulatus sonoriensis,* otherwise known as javelina or peccary. A herd of them scampered across the road in front of us as we bounced over the backlands toward the sea. We stopped and watched them go, crazy as crickets, up a hillside and over the crest, the dust flying from their busy hoofs.

What are javelinas? Piglike animals, but they are not true pigs. They look more like razorback hogs, but they are not true razorbacks either. Someone has likened them to a child's notion of what a pig should look like. They are comical, myopic, vicious and excitable. They have sharp little hoofs, pointed ears, small square bodies and huge heads mounted on massive necks; neck and head appear to take up nearly half the total body volume. The tail is so small as to be ridiculous, but the teeth are sharp. Javelinas are capable (it is said) of inflicting severe—even fatal—damage upon anyone unlucky enough to find himself between a charging javelina and an immovable wall.

I remembered my first encounter with javelinas. I was blundering about in the Sonoran hills, daydreaming as usual, when I gradually became aware of a snorting, snuffling sound ahead, accompanied by the shuffle of many active hoofs. The terrain was brushy, the lilac twilight falling about me, so that I could not see much, and besides I was listening primarily to the melancholy chorus of red-spotted toads in the canyon below. I crashed on through the thickets. The nearsighted javelinas did not notice my approach until I almost stumbled over them. At that point the herd exploded in all directions at once, two of them stampeding past me so close on either side I felt the friction of their bristles. They must have been even more startled than I was. A moment later I stood alone in a now-quiet little clearing, among uprooted roots and overturned stones, and sniffed at the curious musky odor in the air. Off in the distance, at 16 different compass points, I could still hear the panicked scramble, the outraged snorts, squeals and grunts, of the shattered herd of javelinas. It must have taken them hours to get properly reassembled and back to their evening feed.

As with humans and chulus, javelinas will eat anything—snails, locusts, roots, berries, clams, truffles, mushrooms, garlic, bugs, birds, eggs, general assorted garbage. This is reputed to be an indication of intelligence. Living in the Sonoran Desert, however, the javelina specializes in the consumption of cactus—spines, barbs, hooks, needles, thorns, hair and all; its favorite cactus is the succulent pad of the prickly pear.

The javelina also fancies the barrel, or compass, cactus, that bloated monster of a vegetable that rises up like an overgrown green fireplug, leaning south, all over the sunny sides of hills. But the barrel cactus, armored by an intricate network of rosy claws, cannot easily be approached, except for the yellowish fruit on top, which the javelina and other creatures will extricate and consume in due season. The only way a javelina can get at the tender insides of a barrel cactus is from the base, exposed occasionally when excessive growth, or a storm, or a weakened root system, causes the plant to keel over. Then the javelina, seizing its chance, drops to its knees and burrows headfirst into the bottom of the now defenseless plant. I have never actually seen this performance but I have seen barrel cactus fallen over and hollowed out, and all around the scuffle marks and scat of the javelina.

On to the sea. All day long Felger and I rattled through the desert; we passed a few small rancherias where mesquite-branch corrals, idle windmills and small mud huts attested to the part-time presence of our fellow men. But we saw no one. We passed other ranches obviously abandoned. Herds of starving cattle appeared from time to time but not so frequently as north of Caborca.

Ahead the horizon was cactus-studded. Eventually we topped a rise and came to our first cardon, a cactus related to and resembling the Arizona saguaro, but with many more branches, greater mass, a more bronzed, massive and *sculptured* appearance. And "sculptured" seems the best word. The older, properly aged, wind-blasted and sun-scorched cardons do indeed look as if they'd been hammered out of bronze and old iron by some demented junkyard genius from Hoboken, New Jersey. The biggest cardons grow just as tall as the noblest saguaros, maybe a little taller; they must weigh three times as much. In girth, near the base, where all the mighty branches start out, they could equal the biggest oak or cottonwood I ever saw. Like the saguaro, the cardon is basically columnar in structure, with flexible, expansible fluting in trunk and branch to permit gains and losses in moisture content. Compared to the cardon the saguaro seems slender, even graceful, almost elegant; compared to the saguaro the cardon is a crude hulking brute of an organism. I'll take the cardon.

Tastes differ. I asked Dr. Felger to name his favorite vegetable. "I am a scientist," he said. "I refuse to make value judgments." Spoken like a true scientist. Then he added: "They are all my friends."

Finally we went through a pass in the desert hills, and there off on the western horizon lay an infinite band of blue, a misty shimmer of vapor and sky that merged one with the other far off beyond the end of land. We were coming at last to the sea, El Mar de Cortés, or, as it is identified on most maps, the Gulf of California.

As we approached the sea the cacti began to peter out, becoming smaller and sparser. Apparently the damp sea air does not entirely

Not far from its rich larder of fish food in the Gulf of California, an osprey approaches its nest in the coastal Mexican desert. The nest, a bulky affair built of sticks, perches atop a cardon cactus, a Mexican cousin of the saguaro; the cardon can grow 10 feet larger than its stately relative.

agree with them. First the cardons disappeared, then the saguaros, then the others. Last to hold out, sometimes on the dunes behind the beach, were the senita and a few scrubby specimens of cholla.

The road we were following brought us to a fishing village called Puerto Libertad, inhabited by half a dozen families of Seri Indians and on occasion by American tourists and fishermen. We could see the huts of the Indians, at the northern end of the bay, and two houses built by American colonists, near the beach, but since we had no business with any of those people and needed no supplies, we turned south on a road —a single-lane sand track—paralleling the shore.

After a few miles we turned off and took a seaward trail to inspect the beach and the gulf. What we found first was a natural water hole, or *pozo*, within half a mile of the beach. From this water hole, lined with tules and Olney bulrushes, innumerable trails radiated, revealing the visitation of not only the usual starving scrub cattle but also many of the more common desert mammals. I tasted the water: saline, but evidently not so much that the animals would not drink it. At some point the hole or seep had been enlarged and fenced in with a few strands of barbed wire, long since broken through.

Dr. Felger found much of interest around this well: more weeds. But I was aware of something else, something I hadn't heard for nigh on to a year: the clamor of the sea. It came from over the brow of the dunes, where saltbush and marshgrass shivered in the wind, where gulls circled, screaming, where a lone osprey searched for its supper.

I climbed the ridge and descended through hot sand to a splendid beach. The glare of the sun, the glittering waves, dazzled my eyes. A strong wind blew onshore, roiling the water onto the beach; the gush of foam, the steady roar of the waves, the moan of the wind combined in most pleasing symphony, filling the air with that constant vibration of the elements in action.

The beach curved in unbroken crescent north and south, perhaps 15 miles long, empty of any human company. Felger caught up with me and we walked the strand and hunted souvenirs. We found shark eggs, sand dollars, kelp, starfish, rotting sponges, the shell of a fiddler crab. I looked inside: nobody home. We found bleach bottles, tequila bottles, cans, fragments of boat and fishing tackle, and other jetsam, mostly non-biodegradable but all somewhat modified by passage through the salty sea. Strange to find such garbage on this lonely shore. Reassuring, no doubt, to some people: nothing is far away these days.

Better to make camp for the night deep in the cactus land. Bats flickered through the dusk, a horned owl hooted from the top of a nearby cardon, coyotes and bobcats, skunks and badgers, serpents and tarantulas were all on the prowl for supper. We fried our bacon, warmed up our beans, drank our wine and slept.

The next day we took off for points still farther south. We were now entering the most magnificent and varied desert garden I had ever seen. First and predominant were the great cardons, towering 50 and 60 feet. Here and there were the familiar saguaros, organ pipes and senitas, and one new to me, what the Mexicans call *agria,* an ugly, sinister reptilian thing that crawls and twists over the ground in knots with itself. Then there were the many kinds of prickly pear and cholla, including such unusual varieties as Schott's cholla and the purple staghorn cholla, which conceals its chlorophyll beneath a purplish skin.

Some of the agave plants, we noticed when we stopped to inspect them at close range, were about ready to erect their mighty stalks and burst into the one great efflorescence of their glorious and tragic careers. Now is the time, said Dr. Felger, to eat them. When the center leaves begin to part, he explained, that is the time to dig up the agave, cut out its heart, roast the heart on slow coals and eat it. Especially delicious, he continued, when seasoned with a bit of wild garlic—and he knelt and with his fingers dug up a tiny, obscure little green plant that I had not even noticed. He scraped the dirt from the small white bulb at the end of the roots and offered it to me. I ate it. It was good, although it tasted a bit more like scallion than garlic, I thought.

We stayed that evening with friends of Felger's, a missionary couple, in the Seri Indian village of Desemboque near the mouth of the usually dry Río San Ignacio. Beyond the village lay miles of open beach, unimproved by a single visible work of man, curving south toward a craggy headland called Mount Tepoca. Behind the beach were high dunes of white sand, adorned with flowering vines that I could not identify. I wandered across these virgin sands, marveling at their beauty, picking up and casting aside sea shells, each of them a natural work of art. I paused for a good look around. There was the loveliness of the dunes, the sea, the sky; there was the squalid village in the distance, and across the gulf, dimly apparent through the mist and clouds and radiance of the setting sun, rose the dark mountains of Baja California.

The next day we tooled across mile-long ceramic dry lake beds, then through more of the lonely, lovely, delectable wilds, with giant cacti thriving all around and in the background rugged peaks of granite and iron standing against the sky. We were headed for Cape Tepoca and the bay beyond it on the south. Rounding the headland and coming toward the bay, we gained a glorious view of Tiburón Island, itself a half-sunken mountain range surrounded by the waters of the gulf. To the north of Tiburón, I saw a small island that looked much like a pyramid covered with snow, ivory or granulated sugar. A rookery for seabirds, Felger explained; the white stuff is guano.

We left the main road and followed a dirt track that skirted mangrove estuaries, then faded out between the shore and the steep slope of the mountain. There we stopped, and cooked supper beside the shingle beach. As we ate, we watched ponderous pelicans flap in formation above the waves, then peel off and plunge straight down into the water, like dive bombers, and come up with fish. Dolphins passed by some 50 yards offshore. An osprey sailed out from its home in the cactus forest, skimmed over the surface of the water, caught a fish and lugged it through the air back to a shaggy nest on the top of a cardon. Watching the bird through field glasses I saw it tear off and eat the fish's head: always the best part first.

For several days and nights we lounged along that marvelous shore, between the desert and the sea, under the intense sun and splendid light, unknown mountains behind us, equally unknown mountains floating against the sunsets across the gulf. I walked for hours on the golden beach, swam in the cold clear salt water, wandered through the cactus forest. It is the kind of place where you can do absolutely nothing for days on end and only wish you could do even less.

When time came to leave, we drove down the coast road to Kino Bay, then east from Kino to Hermosillo. Back to the human world: miles of smoke, dust, butchered hills, scalped cotton fields and chicken factories, a part of Sonora's brand-new industrial agriculture. Mexico, too, rushes into the future.

I thought of the wilderness we had left behind us, open to sea and sky, joyous in its plenitude, perfect yet vulnerable, unaware of what is coming, defended by nothing, guarded by no one.

7/ The Ancient Dust

There were hills and valleys a-many, of piled-up
hell-fire suddenly grown cold. The lava glowered and
scowled at the heavens and dared us to come on.

WILLIAM T. HORNADAY/ *CAMPFIRES ON DESERT AND LAVA*

Your desert rat is basically just another poor bare forked featherless biped, like the rest of us, but he has certain distinguishing features: a permanent squint, a hide well pricked with cactus acupunctures, the big toes all purple and dead from kicking stones, and inside the skull hardly any viable brains left.

The desert rat loves water but prefers to live, like his four-footed cousin the kangaroo rat, where water is rare as uranium. The rarity makes it precious, therefore lovable. For this rat the finest of all music is the tinkle of seep water trickling into a tin cup, the periodic drip of unseen waterdrops falling in the shadows upon tympanic stone.

He is tolerably adapted to intense heat, constant glare, sand in his eggs, scorpions in his shoes, kissing bugs in his bedroll. He doesn't mind a landscape composed mostly of naked rock with some scrubby-looking plants creeping cautiously out of the cracks; in fact he tends to find green pastures and grassy lawns and trees—especially the fat sort with bushy green foliage—stifling, even claustrophobic. Which brings us to space, outer-inner space, and the desert rat's special fetishes.

He loves all forms of life, even people. But though he loves people (in moderation), he does like to see them, just like trees and bushes, spaced well apart. At a comfortable spitting distance from one another —say two miles, with a sawtooth hogback monocline about a mile high in between for a fence.

This is not meant to suggest that the desert rat is necessarily tougher than other rats. He is certainly not nearly so tough, for example, as the *Rattus rattus urbanus,* that highly specialized breed that thrives or at least survives on cement and steel, clamor and crime, lethal gasoline fumes and the deadly double dry martini. Compared to him the desert rat is a delicate, fastidious epicene, tender as a water lily. But the desert rat carries one distinction like a halo: he has learned to love the kind of country that most people consider unlovable. Call the desert barren, harsh, bitter, dreary and gloomy, acrid and arid, lifeless, hopeless, ugly as sin, foreboding as the gates of Hell—he will happily agree with you. Because in his heart lies the secret conviction that the awful desert is really sweet and lovable, that the ugly is really beautiful, that Hell is Home. And if others think he is crazy so much the better; he is reluctant to share his love anyway.

Even for desert rats, however, there are limits. Some think that the blood-sucking cone-nosed kissing bug is too much of a good thing. Some draw the line at centipedes that drop from the ceiling into your cooking pots. Some hesitate at six-foot diamondbacks coiled on the welcome mat in the evening. But these are petty annoyances. More serious divisions of opinion between desert rats concern places. Some, for example, feel that Death Valley, in the summertime, at 130° F. in the shade, is going too far. Most would agree, however, that the ultimate among the various provinces of The Great American Desert is Sonora's Pinacate region, at the head of the Gulf of California. This region is the bleakest, flattest, hottest, grittiest, grimmest, dreariest, ugliest, most useless, most senseless desert of them all. It is the villian among badlands, most wasted of wastelands, most foreboding of forbidden realms. At least in the Southwest, the Pinacate desert is the final test of desert rathood; it is here that we learn who is a true rat and who is essentially only a desert mouse.

One cannot claim that Pinacate is a scenic area in any common sense of the word. The deserts of northern Arizona and southern Utah feature sheer-walled canyons, thousands of feet deep, entrenched for 500 miles through great plateaus; the biggest "canyon" in Pinacate is a gulch about 40 feet deep and 10 miles long. Almost anywhere else in the Southwest you will see real mountains with snow fields and alpine flora; but in Pinacate country the highest point is Pinacate Peak itself, a tired old dome-shaped volcano (extinct) rising only 3,957 feet above sea level. Hardly enough elevation to cast a shadow or float a cloud. Volcanic phenomena are a Pinacate specialty, but even in this aspect its cinder cones, craters and lava flows do not equal in color and drama those of the Sunset Crater volcanic region of northern Arizona.

Well then, you ask, what *is* the attraction? Why should anyone go out of his way to contemplate the Pinacate country, El Gran Desierto, this ultimate wasteland?

One answer might be that very few people ever do go out there. A few Mexican woodcutters; a few hardened hot-country fanatics from the States. But this is not an answer, only an evasion. Perhaps the explanation is that the appeal of the Pinacate country lies in its total lack of any obvious appeal. In its emptiness. In its vast, desolate nothingness. At its heart is a 750-square-mile volcanic field, an iron-hard iron-hued wilderness of craters, cones, congealed lava flows, with tired old Pinacate Peak in the middle. To the south lie the empty salt marshes, the sandy hummocks that border the Gulf of California coast. On the north and east are rugged little granite ranges and more cactus and creosote desert, inhabited only by a few starving scrub cattle and wild animals. On the outskirts of this desert are the towns of Sonoita, San Luisito, and Puerto Peñasco, with a combined population of maybe 60,000 people. Which isn't much for an area the size of Connecticut.

And then there is the erg.

The erg (a term borrowed from the Arabic) is a sea of sand, an ocean of dunes stretching from the base of Pinacate Peak all the way to what is left of the Colorado River and its now mostly lifeless delta at the head of the gulf. From peak to delta is a distance of about a hundred miles by line of sight, interrupted only by a few small, isolated, waterless desert mountains. In all of the region there is nothing that can be called man-made except the highway skirting its northern edge and on the south the single railway line that runs along the coast from Mexicali to Puerto Peñasco.

The sand dunes, like the volcanic field and the glittering sea that form so much of the horizon here, have one quality more overwhelming than any other: a great brooding solemnity, compounded of equal parts of distance, space, emptiness and silence. "Nothing is more real than nothing," wrote Samuel Beckett, thinking of the human soul; he could have said it of Pinacate. Thomas Hardy, too, would have found something familiar in this moorland among deserts. And desert rats, like all romantics, are half in love with that abyss that yawns over yonder, beyond the world's rim.

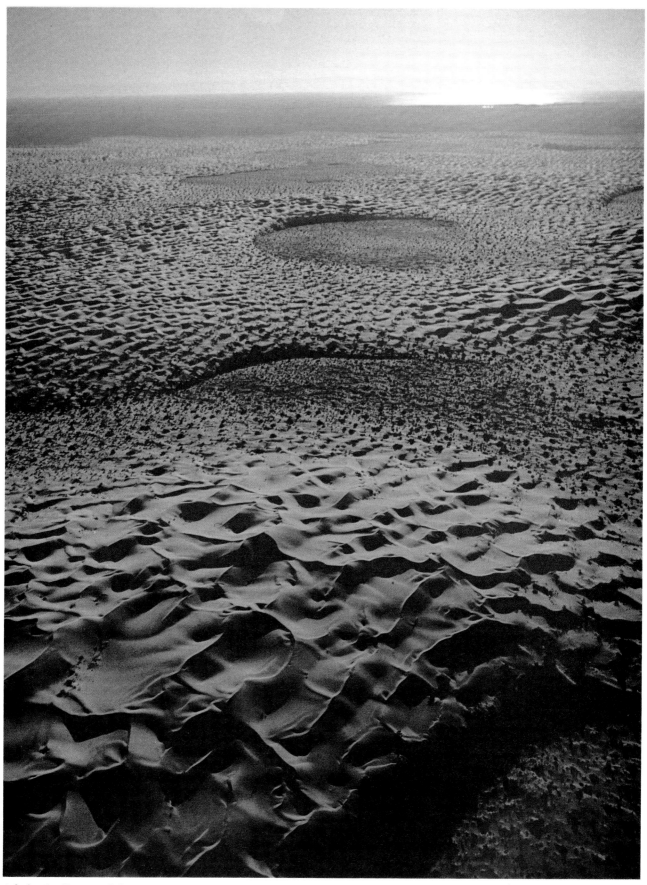

A belt of rolling sand dunes, as much as 40 miles wide in places, borders the Gulf of California in Mexico's Gran Desierto.

"There's something about the desert," a friend once said to me, trying to explain why he loved the desert. Rather, why he loved it so *much*. And try though he would, he could say no more. I have often wondered what the answer would have been from one of the most famous of Death Valley oldtimers, a prospector named Seldom Seen Slim. But he never answered his telephone. He didn't have a telephone. And he was never home. Didn't have a home.

I have tried to analyze my own emotions on this subject: why am I so much in love with the desert? I love also the sea and the seashore, the mountains, lakes and glaciers, the soft blue-green hills of my Appalachian boyhood, the plains of Oklahoma, the blue grottoes of Capri, the dark forests of Bavaria, the misty golden hills of Scotland, yes, even the back alleys of Hoboken, New York City, Berlin, Naples, Barcelona, Brisbane, Pittsburgh. There's beauty, heartbreaking beauty, everywhere. Still, after all, when I think of where I want to be, in the end it's the old hot dusty eyeball-searing head-aching skin-blistering throat-parching boot-burning bloody goddamned desert. Why?

"There's something about the desert . . ." my friend had said. And paused. And halted. And could say no more. He might of course have mentioned the obvious things: the bracing aridity of the air, the clarity of the light (where industry has not yet shoved its brutal snout into the hinterlands), the elegant neoclassic simplicity of the landscape, the landforms, the relative scarcity of man and his works, the queerness of the plant life, the admirable hardiness of the animal life, the splendor of sundown after an August storm, the rare oracular miracle of dripping springs in a nearly waterless land, the human history—the Indians fighting against cruel and hopeless odds, the Euro-American whites driving onward the frontiers of expanding empire. All of this is true enough, but every other particular region, anywhere on earth, has its distinctive features too.

Yet none quite fulfills the peculiar appeal that the desert scene has for some of us. There is something more in the desert, something that has no name. I might call it a mystery—or simply Mystery itself, with a capital "M." Unlike forest or seashore, mountain or city, plain or swamp, the desert, any desert, suggests always the promise of something unforeseeable, unknown but desirable, waiting around the next turn in the canyon wall, over the next ridge or mesa, somewhere within the wrinkled hills. What, exactly? Well . . . a sort of treasure. A kind of delight. God? Perhaps. Gold? Maybe. Grace? Possibly. But something a little more, a little different, even from these.

So there you are. The secret revealed, the essence uncovered, we come right back to where we started. The desert rat loves the desert because there is something about it that he cannot explain or even name.

Which brings us full wobbly circle back to Pinacate, because here is the secret allure of the desert in its purest form—simply because there is so little to compete with it: no great canyons, no mighty mountains, no spectacular flora or fauna, no weird and colorful rock formations, no winy spirits in the air. Only the bleak and brooding badlands, the shimmering sea of sand, the watery rim of the salt sea.

After the generalizations come the qualifications. As I have noted, the plant life in the Pinacate country is sparse. But the first time I visited this area was in March of 1968, which was a great year for desert wild flowers; the winter rains had come in just the right amounts and at proper intervals. Guided by ranger-naturalist Bill Hoy, our party approached from the east, off the Puerto Peñasco road, and drove to the end of a woodcutters' truck road at a waterless dead end called Paloverde Camp. Except for the lone paloverde that gave the place its name, there was a dearth of shade as well as of water; even in March the daytime temperature was in the high 80s.

But this mattered little. What we saw, looking up from that forlorn spot among the rocks, was the 2,000-foot-high slope of a cindery mountain all covered with a rash, a fuzzy golden coat, of blooming brittlebush, *Encelia farinosa*, yellow flowers spread across a panorama 20 miles wide. Proceeding on foot, we found other early spring flowers in bloom: the pinkish fairy duster, or *Calliandra eriophylla*: the golden Mexican poppy, *Escholtzia mexicana*; the scarlet-flowered hummingbird's trumpet bush, *Zauschneria californica*; and the coral-colored globe mallow, *Sphaeralcea ambigua*. Masses of bloom. Drunken honeybees, sick with joy, zigzagged crazily from bush to bush, flower to flower, having the time of their lives.

That was the day Bill Hoy rappelled down into the well-like opening of a 60-foot fumarole in the heart of a lava flow and almost failed to come back. We watched him go down—his Argentine wife, Marina, a friend, myself—and saw him fade into the gloom at the bottom of the fumarole. He poked around for a while in the ancient dust, hoping to find Indian artifacts, the pelvic bones of sacrificial virgins, a further opening to the underworld, anything novel, literary, scientific. There was nothing but darkness and dust.

He started back up the rope, pulling himself upward and out with the aid of a pair of jumars—clamplike metal devices that grip a rope with many times the leverage of human hands. This particular fumarole, however, has a pronounced overhang on its inside rim. When Bill reached it he found himself hung up. His weight pulled the rope tight against the face of the overhang so that he couldn't move the clamps up the line. He was dangling, and could not claw his way around the overhang. Nor could we risk pulling him from the top by the upper end of the rope, even though it was firmly attached to a rock near the rim of the fumarole. Bill's weight on the rope, its friction on the rock and the added strain of our tugging from above might have broken the line. The only thing we could do was lower a second line. Long, sweaty, hard-breathing minutes followed, while we let down the second rope, and Bill succeeded—one-handed—in securing it around his chest. We had him belayed. Then we pulled him out into the middle of the fumarole and away from the overhang, so he was able to use his jumars, and clamber over the lip of rock.

Next day we visited Crater Elegante, the deepest and one of the most spectacular of Pinacate's collapse calderas, to use the precise geological term, formed by the sinking of subsurface magma. The result in the case of this caldera is an almost perfectly circular depression over a mile in diameter and approximately 850 feet deep. The walls slope at a moderate grade, so that it is possible to scramble down to the interior. Here you find a sparse growth of typical Sonoran Desert shrubbery —creosote bush and cactus—and a small population of mice and lizards and birds. There is no permanent water in Crater Elegante; the inhabitants therefore must manufacture their own water, metabolically, as kangaroo rats do, for example, or obtain it from the blood and tissue of their occasional prey.

We left the volcanic field by a northerly route, skirting the frontal edge of a lava flow 50 feet high and several miles long. Here too the brittle-bush was in massed bloom, and under the flowers we glimpsed the collared lizard, the leopard lizard and the fat chuckwalla, once much prized by Papago gourmets. A fierce-looking lizard a foot long, the chuckwalla will, when threatened, crawl into a rock crevice and inflate itself, wedging its body tightly in place. This helps as defense against hawks and coyotes but not against hungry Indians. The Papago would deflate the lizard with a knife or sharpened stick and drag it out, squirming, to meet its fate. Which was not good, from the chuckwalla's point of view: it would be boiled alive, like a lobster, or eaten raw.

Among the Indians and Mexicans of Sonora the Pinacate desert is considered a *mal país,* an evil land, a place better to be avoided.

The dangers once were quite tangible. More than a century ago Pinacate was the territory of the Pinacateño Areñero, a subgroup of the Indian tribe known as Sand Papago. They were thought by other Indians to be proficient in the magical arts, especially the malevolent variety. Whether this was so or not, the Pinacateño were definitely hostile toward outsiders, perhaps because their homeland was so hostile to them. Dependent for survival upon the meager fruits of cactus and mesquite and such scattered, hard-to-take game as bighorn sheep, jack rabbits and whitetail deer, they understandably resented intruders: more competition for an already marginal food supply.

When strangers did appear, passing through or along the edges of Pinacate toward El Dorado of Southern California, the Pinacateño ambushed them at the few water holes. Many missionaries, traders, gold seekers and other travelers died in the blue hours of dawn, their bodies studded with arrows, their guns not even in their hands. But as always the white men soon got the best of the Indians: most of the Pinacateño died of yellow fever in the 1850s, and only 30 to 40 descendants—none of them full-blooded—survive.

Today the vestiges of the Indians and traces of their forebears who roamed the region for thousands of years before can still be seen. It was they who made the delicate but definite pathways that follow the contours of the land and wind across the level desert. Near the *tinajas,* or natural water tanks, of the area you will see potsherds; if you are lucky you may find, hidden among the rocks, a complete clay pot, intact. Out in the open, along the ancient foot trails that lead from water hole to water hole, from the hills to the dunes, from the desert to the sea, is other evidence of the former inhabitants: heaps of broken sea shells, cairns that may have been trail shrines, campground clearings and sleeping circles. The latter are small cleared places on the ground, enclosed, sometimes only partially, by low stone walls that functioned as windbreaks; despite the intense heat of the days the nights can be cold in the Pinacate desert, especially when a wind is blowing. These Indians may or may not have had blankets; they probably kept themselves warm at night with one another's bodies—"body heaps."

Even if the Pinacateño had never lived here, there is something about the region itself—the grim landscape, the iron hills and bluish basaltic arroyos, the brooding sky, the scarcity of even the simplest forms of life—to suggest magic to a certain cast of mind, thoughts of the supernatural and the occult. It's the kind of country old veteran witch doctors would like.

I found myself thinking about this on our second trip to the Pinacate country, a year after the first, in the awful heat of May. We came down from Los Vidrios on the north for a look at the western side of the desert, and on the way we stopped near what appeared to be no more than a modest rise. We climbed it and found ourselves peering down into a ghastly pit of jagged black basalt 650 feet deep. Sykes Crater. Much wider than it is deep, this crater makes a more vivid impression on the senses than the more accessible expanse of Crater Elegante. Here at Sykes the precipitous walls, the pitlike proportions, the angular exposure of the rock, the shadowy depths, combine to suggest something hostile, evil, the ruthless violence of the underworld's mostly dormant but always potent vulcanism.

From Sykes Crater, we drove southward for some 20 miles and three hours over the roughest, rockiest jeep trail this side of Baja California. Eventually we reached the dead end of the trail at a place called Tule Tank, where we made camp for several days and nights.

Tule Tank isn't much to look at, merely a bench of lava rock with some scrubby paloverde and saguaro growing out of it, low buttes and ridges forming the horizon, but in the gulch close by is one of the few usually reliable *tinajas* in the entire region, a deeply corroded watertight basin in the basalt bedrock. It is not a spring; there are no springs in Pinacate. The *tinaja* is filled by thunderstorms and flash floods, after which it may be 10 to 15 feet deep, depending upon the amount of gravel and rocks washed into the tank. Because of the high walls on either side, which shade it from the sun and retard evaporation, this *tinaja* almost always contains some water.

A few words on water-hole etiquette: where they are rare, as in Pinacate, it is considered bad form to bathe in *tinajas*, especially by the next person who comes along needing a drink. A good desert rat prefers to scrub himself with sand and sunshine anyway.

Once comfortably set up in the shade, what there was of it, with a couple of canvas bags of *tinaja* water hanging from a limb of a paloverde, evaporating and cooling in the hot breeze, we began to think about climbing a mountain, such as it is, i.e., Pinacate Peak. There wasn't any other mountain immediately available. We thought about it all day long, reclining in the shade with our bird books and lizard books, waiting for the sun to decline to a bearable angle. In the evening we went for a long walk over the flats and thought about it some more. Off

Nearly a mile across and 450 feet deep, MacDougal Crater in the Pinacates supports a growth of plants where a volcano once spewed fire.

in the west, paralleling the rim of the sea, the rippled erg glimmered at us, blazing with light and heat, endless and depthless. Perhaps we should investigate the dune world. We strolled across the desert pavement, under a fat rising moon, and thought about the moon and the dunes and the mountain.

Desert pavement is aptly named. Very small volcanic stones and cinders, worn smooth as tile by millennia of weathering and closely packed in a matrix of silt, form a regular, level surface where few plants ever gain even a nominal foothold. Chemical reactions among soil, rock and air, continuing through the centuries, have given the "pavement" a varnishlike patina of black. Some of these pavements extend for a mile, as wide as they are long, God's own natural parking lots for spiritual shopping centers.

The old fool moon drifted along above, soft and silvery and well worn as a peon's last peso, shedding its indifferent light upon the grand desolation around us. Pinacate, the sleeping volcano, sloped upward on the east, half in moonlight, half in shadow. Becking? Not really.

A "moonbird" called from some dark crevice in the fractured lava: "Poor-will . . . poor-will . . . poor-will. . . ." The Southwest's small relative of the Eastern whippoorwill, the moonbird or poorwill or *Phalaenoptilus nuttallii* has kept me awake for half of many a desert night. Especially when the moon was up. The only recourse is to crawl out of your sack and pitch rocks at the bastard till it flutters off to go haunt somebody else for a while.

Risky, though. There's something a little weird, a bit supernatural about those moonbirds, most of all when heard in the eerie emptiness of the Pinacate country. We looked again at the mountain. One way to exorcise any evil spirits here might be through direct confrontation, face to face, human to inhuman, upon the summit of their territory.

We would climb the mountain. Why not?

But first we spent a day out on the billowing sea of sand, a picnic in the erg. The only erg in the Western Hemisphere, someone told me once. Which may well be true. Arabia, the Sahara, that is where ergs belong. We jounced down the trail in our hardy Toyota, following a sandy wash under giant mesquites and lovely graceful paloverdes covered with the golden bloom of spring toward those pale brownish yellowish reddish dunes that rimmed the western horizon. (The color of them changes from hour to hour, from place to place, with the declensions of the sun.) A few miles to the north were granitic mountains, low but rugged, all rock, like miniature Tetons, half buried by the encroaching sand. Nobody lives out there but a few bighorn sheep, the usual rats, lizards, birds and snakes. The sand became deeper and softer, too much even for four-wheel drive. We got out, shouldered our packs, and marched out of the shade and into the heat, out and up and into the erg.

On the dunes nothing is simple. From the distance we had seen nothing but sand. But once out on it, in it, we discovered forms and signs of life everywhere. Most worthy of honorable mention were the mesquite trees, small and scattered but quite beautiful in their fresh green spring leafery; they too were in bloom, with a fragrance faint but sweet, smelling like apples. We saw saltbush, the four-winged variety, and clumps of smoke tree, that ghostly shrub. There was locoweed, sand verbena, coyote gourd and other plants I could not recognize. Occasionally we saw dead trees, both mesquite and paloverde, which had been smothered by parasitic mistletoe. All over the sand were the tracks of rats, mice, lizards, birds, snakes, beetles and butterflies. Butterfly tracks? Why not? Butterflies have feet too, just like you and me.

We saw all of this on the edges of the erg. As we tramped farther in, following the cornices of the great firm dunes, the plant life and with it the animal life became more and more scarce, until finally, maybe a mile into that silent oven of sand and sky and sun, we came to where there was no more life. Except us, alien and awed.

A zephyr of wind came up, stirred the loose fine sand on the immaculate edge of the dune we stood on, and pushed it over the brink. Lying on our bellies, we could hear a delicate tinkling sound as the grains of sand drifted off the cornice and tumbled down the slip face of the dune. We rolled over and looked up at the sky, that mad dome of blue with its solitary fanatic star. I let my head hang back over the edge of the dune and studied the world upside down. Always a wise and refreshing practice.

About then I noticed two pairs of black wings soaring casually, nonchalantly, without effort, somewhere halfway between us and the sun. Vultures. Patient, and hungry as always. We decided to get back to camp before our brains got roasted and our eyeballs plucked.

Next day we climbed the mountain. No great climb, really, not even a scramble, just a long hike, up the lower slopes and up a ravine where we passed La Tinaja Alta, the highest natural water tank in Pinacate. We noticed as we trudged by that it contained only a few inches of water. We took a long thirsty pull—from our canteens instead—left the ravine and began the tedious ascent of the peak. Hot up there; gravity dragged at our boots. Through scattered saguaros, stands of shiny teddy bear cholla, we tramped on, crazy as crickets—"Why are we doing this?" "My God I don't know, why are you doing it?" "My God, I don't know, I guess I'm crazy, what's your excuse?"—until, four hours from Tule Tank, we reached the summit of Pinacate Peak.

There was nobody there but us mountain climbers. No gods, no spirits, no ghosts that I could see, only the wind and the brittlebush and a great deal of loose scaly rock.

It was not even a first, our conquest of the mountain. We found a canister and inside it a register book filled with names and dates: half the hiking clubs of Southern California had been here before us. Also the third-best lady mountain climber of Arizona. We added our names to the list. Half the point of climbing a mountain is to be able to say you did it; the other half is getting back down.

But first we took a good survey of the world around us. Even though it was a hazy day we still could see for close to 50 miles in all directions. There was obvious Arizona on the north, mantled in smelter smog and progress, as usual. The state of Sonora to the east did not look much healthier. South we could see a range of granitic mountains called Sierra Blanca; a friend named Larry May, an ecologist and a hopeless, incurable desert rat, would take me there later to show me a valley where he had measured the temperature, one day in June 1971, at 134°F., which equals the highest reading ever recorded at Death Valley and is close to the world record of 136° taken at a weather station called Azizia in Libya.

We gazed southwest and west, beyond the craters and the cones toward the erg, which forms a golden crescent on the verge of the sea. Both the blue sea and the sea of sand extended farther than our vision could carry, fading off into the western haze and a vague suggestion of the mountains of Baja California.

We descended, down the broken rock and unstable cinders, through the ocotillo jungles and the saguaro groves. Here and there little mahogany pellets, sure sign of bighorn sheep. But the pellets were old, and dry as dust. Are there any bighorns left in this place? I don't know; Larry May says there are. Even mountain lions, or at least a transient mountain lion—he saw it.

The heat became greater as we went down, down from the mountain into the waiting inferno. In the middle of the afternoon we paused for an hour's rest in the shade of an ironwood by the side of La Tinaja

Alta, the high tank. It seemed to us that the water in the little basin had gone down since we had seen it last, two or three hours earlier. We stared at the stagnant oily water, its surface coated with dove feathers and a scum of dust and dead and living bugs, bees, flies, fleas. After the climb, our canteens were empty. The water looked good. We drank some and felt much better.

It was most excellent to lie there on the cool blue-gray basalt under the tough old tree—ironwoods may be almost as long-lived as Methuselah—and watch the bees buzzing and sipping at the water's edge. The heat and glare beyond our little sheltering bower was terrific, stunning, exhausting; the heat waves looked dense enough to float a boat on. But here in the shade we knew peace of a sort, a happy bliss, ease of limb and mind. While my companion filled his canteen, straining the insect-filled tepid water through a bandana, I watched the insouciant birds creeping and flitting through the brush. *Phainopepla nitens, Pyrrhuloxia sinuata, Pipilo fuscus,* all my desert favorites were there, stoking their furious metabolisms with bug and seed, stuffing their greedy gizzards.

We prepared to go, but paused for a last look at the little water hole. Our drink and filling one canteen had plainly lowered the water level another two inches. Only a bucketful or so remained. La Tinaja Alta is a very small *tinaja* to begin with and this was the dry season. The bees crawled over the damp rim of the basin, bedraggled and puzzled. Now the bird cries seemed forlorn.

Out in the rocks and brush somewhere crouched other small animals waiting for us to leave, waiting their turn for a drink. We didn't see them, we didn't hear them, but we felt them.

Four miles to go, a good two hours' march (on that terrain) before we reached camp and the big *tinaja* of Tule Tank. We thought about the birds and bees and animals, the injustice of life, the general harshness of existence. I know, it's tough all over, but nowhere tougher than on the blackened slopes of Pinacate, under that pitiless Sonoran sun.

All the water we had was in the one canteen. We emptied it back into the little stony basin. Not in charity but out of caution. It seemed, after all, no more than a prudent sacrifice to the spirit of the desert.

Rock, Sand and Solitude

PHOTOGRAPHS BY ERNST HAAS

Long an ardent desert buff, photographer Ernst Haas was drawn to El Gran Desierto in Mexico by its reputation as the emptiest, grimmest part of the vast Sonoran Desert. Haas confirmed the superlatives after a two-week trek through hundreds of square miles of barren, jagged mountains, shiny black lava fields and enormous sand dunes. "But," he added, "my strongest impression was of strange, solemn beauty and immutable peace."

According to plan, Haas met his young desert guide, and the two men set out across the moonlike wasteland in late November, when the weather promised nothing worse than chilling nights and midday temperatures in the 80s. Their trip soon settled into an easy routine. They would set up camp for a day or two and explore on foot for miles around. Then they would drive on to a new campsite in a versatile vehicle that was equally capable of traversing razor-sharp lava beds and climbing steep sand dunes.

With only a drizzle and a rainbow as brief diversions, Haas grew increasingly aware of the desert's brooding majesty and disconcerting size. A caldera that seemed merely large from a distance proved to measure three miles around. Every vista was immense and remote, and in scanning the void for a typical plant or an unusual lava formation Haas found himself observing more acutely than ever before. As he later explained, "If you look at nothing long enough, you see something, and it is beautiful."

Always the desert posed picture-taking problems. The blinding glare of the sun in a bleached cloudless sky limited Haas's working day to early morning and late afternoon. Yet even in those periods, deep shadows and the ruddy light played tricks with his subjects, distorting their usual shapes and disguising their somber colors.

And above all there was the silence and solitude. Haas had expected the days of lonely work to make him eager each night for campfire conversation—just for the sheer relief of hearing another human voice. But he and his guide—by tacit agreement—talked less and less as the two weeks passed. Haas felt himself sinking deeper and deeper into a mood of isolation—and enjoying the sensation more and more. When the time came to go back to the frantic pace of the crowded city, he felt altogether refreshed and renewed.

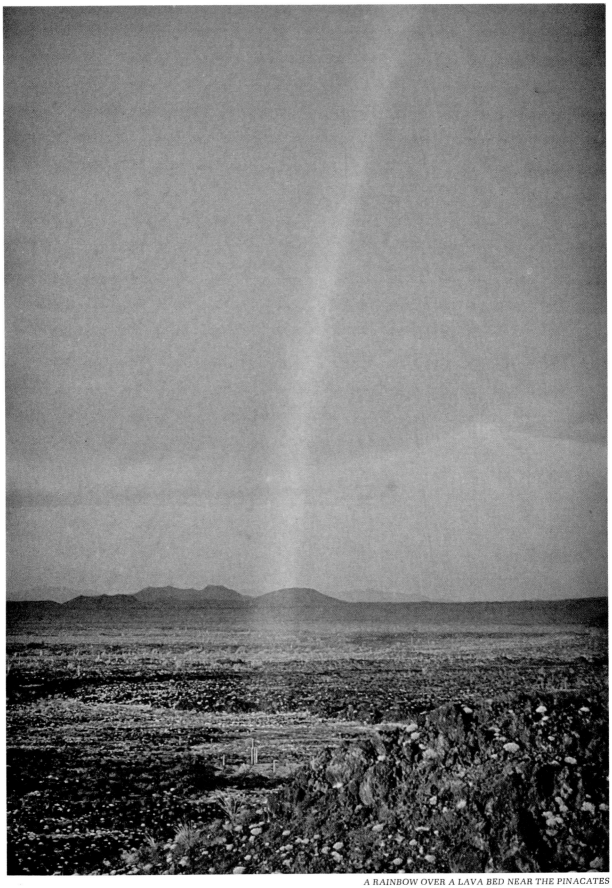

A RAINBOW OVER A LAVA BED NEAR THE PINACATES

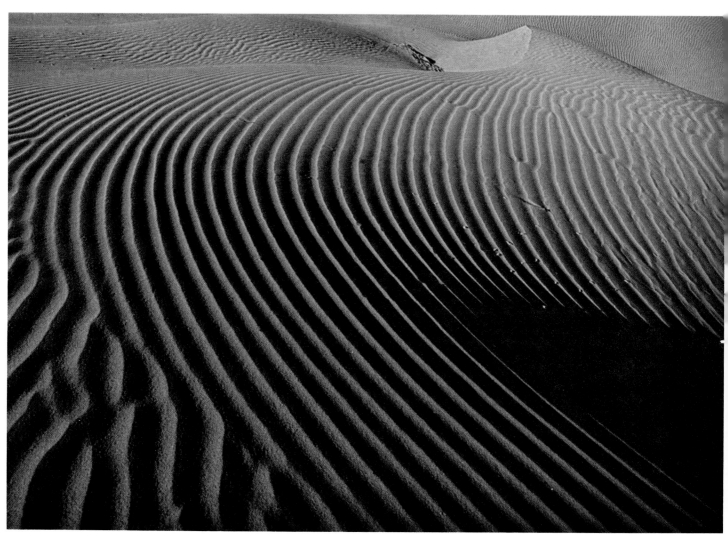

WIND-RIPPLED SAND IN A SEA OF DUNES

A SUN-WASHED OCOTILLO SHRUB

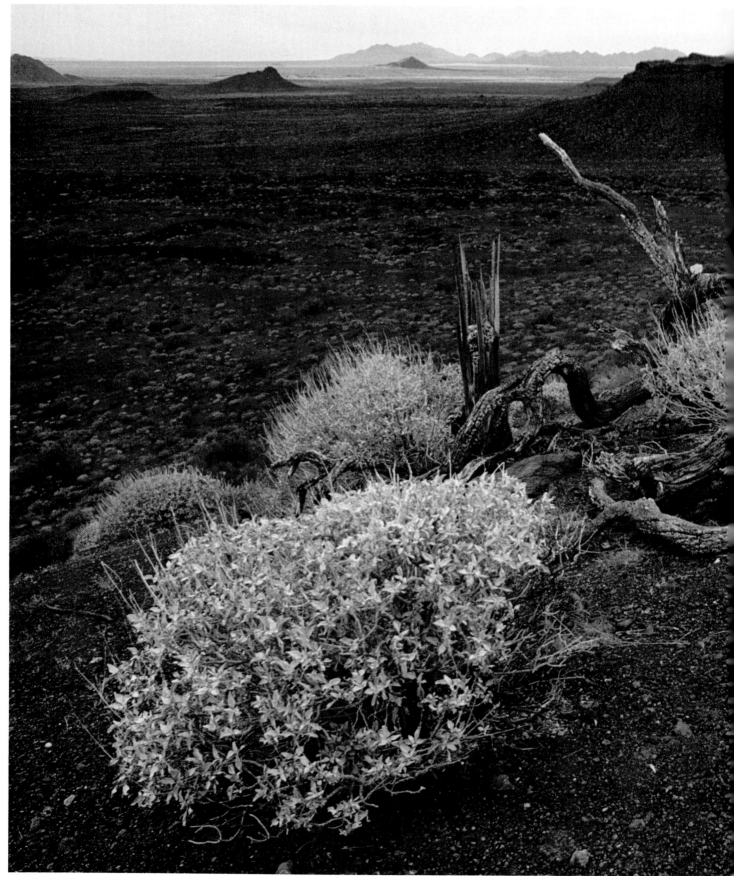

BRITTLEBUSH (FOREGROUND) AND LIMBER BUSH GROWING IN VOLCANIC CINDERS

A PATTERN OF SAND DUNES

WHITE BRITTLEBUSH AMID CREOSOTE SHRUBS

A SHRUB-STUDDED CRATER IN THE PINACATE REGION

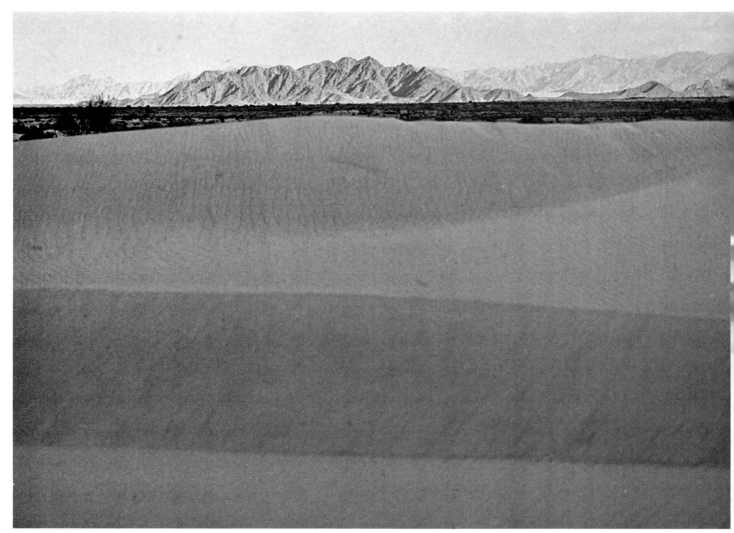

THE ''STANDING WAVE'' DUNES NEAR THE HORNADAY MOUNTAINS

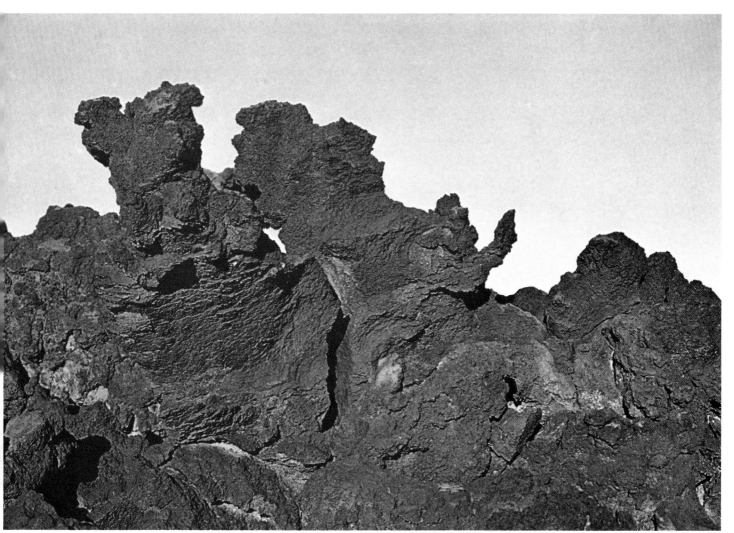

A LAVA FORMATION NEAR MAC DOUGAL CRATER

THE PINACATE BEETLE AND ITS TRACKS

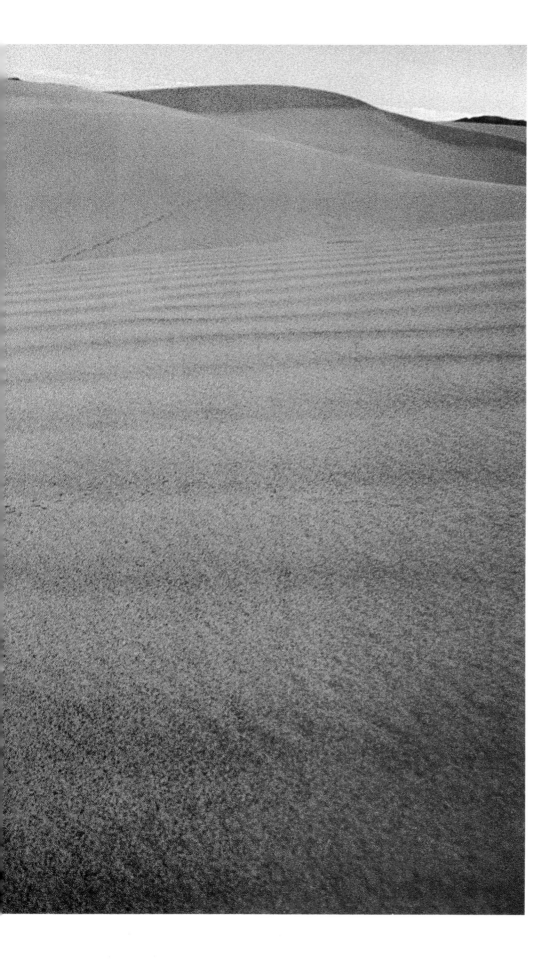

Bibliography

Barnes, William C., *Arizona Place Names*. University of Arizona Press, 1960.

Bates, Marston, *Animal Worlds*. Random House, 1963.

Benson, Lyman, *The Cacti of Arizona* (3rd ed.). University of Arizona Press, 1969.

Borror, Donald J., and Richard E. White, *A Field Guide to the Insects of America North of Mexico*. Houghton Mifflin, 1970.

Dodge, Natt N., *100 Desert Wildflowers in Natural Color*. Southwest Parks and Monuments Association, 1963.

Dodge, Natt N., *Poisonous Dwellers of the Desert* (16th ed.). Southwest Parks and Monuments Association, 1976.

Dodge, Natt N., and Jeanne R. Janish, *Flowers of the Southwest Deserts* (9th ed.). Southwest Parks and Monuments Association, 1976.

Dunbier, Roger, *The Sonoran Desert*. The University of Arizona Press, 1968.

Earle, W. Hubert, *Cacti of the Southwest*. Arizona Cactus and Native Flora Society, 1963.

Gentry, Curt, *The Killer Mountains*. Comstock, 1976.

Hastings, James Rodney, and Raymond M. Turner, *The Changing Mile*. University of Arizona Press, 1965.

Howes, Paul Griswold, *The Giant Cactus Forest and Its World*. Duell, Sloan and Pearce; Little, Brown, 1954.

Jaeger, Edmund C., *Desert Wild Flowers*. Stanford University Press, 1967.

Jaeger, Edmund C., *Desert Wildlife*. Stanford University Press, 1961.

Jaeger, Edmund C., *The North American Deserts*. Stanford University Press, 1957.

Kearney, Thomas H., and Robert H. Peebles, *Arizona Flora*. University of California Press, 1960.

Klauber, Laurence M., *Rattlesnakes* (2 vols.). University of California Press, 1973.

Klots, Alexander B., *A Field Guide to the Butterflies of North America, East of the Great Plains*. Houghton Mifflin, 1977.

Klots, Alexander and Elsie, *Insects of North America*. Doubleday, 1971.

Krutch, Joseph Wood, *The Desert Year*. Penguin, 1977.

Krutch, Joseph Wood, *The Voice of the Desert*. William Morrow, 1955.

Larson, Peggy, *Deserts of America*. Prentice-Hall, 1970.

Leopold, A. Starker, *The Desert* (rev. ed.). Time-Life Books, 1967.

Manning, Reg, *The Cactus Book*. Reganson Cartoon Books, 1969.

Murphy, Robert, *Wild Sanctuaries*. E. P. Dutton, 1968.

Olin, George, *Mammals of the Southwest Deserts* (2nd ed. rev.). Southwest Parks and Monuments Association, 1959.

Peattie, Donald Culross, *A Natural History of Western Trees*. Houghton Mifflin, 1953.

Peterson, Roger Tory, *A Field Guide to Western Birds*. Houghton Mifflin, 1972.

Schmidt-Nielsen, Knut, *Desert Animals: Physiological Problems of Heat and Water*. Dover, 1979.

Shreve, Forrest, and Ira L. Wiggins, *Vegetation and Flora of the Sonoran Desert* (2 vols.). Stanford University Press, 1964.

Sloane, Howard and Lucille, *A Pictorial History of American Mining*. Crown, 1970.

Smith, Hobart M., *Handbook of Lizards*. Comstock, 1946.

Stebbins, Robert C., *A Field Guide to Western Reptiles and Amphibians*. Houghton Mifflin, 1966.

Wallace, Andrew, *The Image of Arizona*. University of New Mexico Press, 1971.

Welles, Philip, *Meet the Southwest Deserts*. Dale Stuart King, 1964.

Woodin, Ann, *Home Is the Desert*. Collier Books, 1970.

Writers' Project, *Arizona* (rev. ed.). Hastings House, 1966.

Acknowledgments

The editors of this book wish to thank the following persons. At the Arizona-Sonora Desert Museum, Tucson: Betty Berg, Executive Secretary; Robert Craig, General Curator; Donald Ducote, Curator of Plants; Charles L. Hanson, Curator of Birds and Mammals; Merritt S. Keasey III, Curator of Small Animals; Larry May, Research Associate; Gale Monson, Resident Supervisor; William H. Woodin, Director Emeritus. At Organ Pipe Cactus National Monument: Karon Begeman, Park Aid; Rothwell P. Broyles, Chief of Interpretation and Resource Management; Larry Henderson, Assistant Chief of Interpretation and Resource Management; Ray G. Martinez Jr., Superintendent; Matt H. Ryan, former Superintendent. Also, Jim Carrico, Superintendent, Great Sand Dunes National Monument, Alamosa, Colorado; Harold T. Coss, Park Interpreter, Saguaro National Monument, Tucson; John DePuy, Oracle, Arizona; Gerald Duncan, Acting Refuge Manager, Kofa Game Range; Richard Felger, Tucson; Sidney S. Horenstein, Department of Invertebrate Paleontology, The American Museum of Natural History, New York; Bill Hoy, Fort Bowie National Historic Site, Willcox, Arizona; Ned Jackson, Recreation and Land Staff Officer, Tonto National Forest, Dr. William H. Loery, Pathologist, Medical Center at Princeton, New Jersey; Larry G. Pardue, The New York Botanical Garden, New York; Douglas Peacock, Tucson; Ann Schlumberger, Tucson; Margaret Sparks, Arizona Pioneers Historical Society, Tucson; Floyd Werner, Professor of Entomology, University of Arizona, Tucson; Ann Woodin, Tucson; John Woodin, Tucson.

Picture Credits

Index